DIGGING INTO THE WORD

DIGGING INTO THE WORD

Kingdom Lessons 1 

Olayiwola Michael

Worldwide Prophetic Evangelical Ministries

CONTENTS

1 Fulfilling Your Purpose 1

2 Be Diligent! 7

3 The Soul that Sinneth Shall Die 11

4 Witnesses that Jesus is the Son of God 15

5 The Judgment Seat of Christ 18

6 Great Things He Has Done 22

7 The Unveiling of the Mystery 24

8 Conquering Fear and Activating God-Given Gifts 27

9 Offer the Sacrifices of Righteousness 29

10 Diligently Seek God 31

11 Honor in Eternity 34

12 Honor in Eternity II 38

CONTENTS

13 | Embracing Jesus: The Divine Creator and Sustainer of Life 43

14 | The Power of Counsel 50

15 | Blessed are the Peacemakers 54

16 | Bringing Forth the Fruits of the Kingdom 58

17 | Lusts and the Renewed Mind 62

18 | The Power of a Renewed Mind 68

19 | The Heavens Rule 72

20 | Faith Like My Chocolate Cake 77

21 | The Stone Was Rolled Away 80

22 | Beware of Flattery 83

23 | Buy the Truth and Receive Freedom through Repentance 86

24 | You Don't Have to Die: Embrace the Giver of Eternal Life and Live 90

25 | Lewd Fellows of a Baser Sort 93

26 | Who Are Liars? 95

27 | Confidence in God 98

28 Expressing Gratitude for the Father's Blessings 102

29 Away with Him, Away with Him! 106

30 The Consequences of Pride and Presumptuous Sin 111

31 Repent and Give your Life to Jesus 114

Fulfilling Your Purpose

A child of God was created in Christ Jesus for good works,
just as a fruit tree was created to bear fruit.

You do not have to perform any good works to come to Jesus, except to believe in Him and repent of your sins, as Ephesians 2:8 states: "For by grace are ye saved through faith; and that not of yourselves: it is the gift of God; 9 Not of works, lest any man should boast."

When you come to Jesus, you should walk in good works, as Ephesians 2:10 explains: "For we are His workmanship, created in Christ Jesus unto good works, which God hath before ordained that we should walk in them." This is not just a commandment for believers; it is the purpose of every believer.

An apple tree was created to produce apples.
An orange tree was created to bear oranges.
And a child of God was created in Christ Jesus to walk in good works.

Good works encompass not only acts like baking a cake for your grandmother, giving flowers to your neighbor, feeding the hungry, clothing the naked, or sheltering the homeless but also refraining from defrauding fellow believers and avoiding actions that harm the work of God.

Good works are synonymous with bearing good fruits, doing good, and abstaining from sin. This is why the first thing God mentions to each of the seven churches in the Book of Revelation is, "I know your works." Works are crucial for salvation, but they must be good. Therefore, if your works are not good, where do you think you will spend eternity?

Matthew 3:10 tells us, "And now also the axe is laid unto the root of the trees: therefore every tree which bringeth not forth good fruit is hewn down and cast into the fire."

John 5:28-29 tells us, "Marvel not at this: for the hour is coming, in which all that are in the graves shall hear His voice, 29 And shall come forth; they that have done good, unto the resurrection of life; and they that have done evil, unto the resurrection of damnation."

In addition, Revelation 22:14-15 tells us, "Blessed are they that do His commandments, that they may have the right to the tree of life and may enter through the gates into the city. 15 For without are dogs, and sorcerers, and whoremongers, and murderers, and idolaters, and whosoever loveth and maketh a lie."

There is honor in eternity for all children of God who do good in the eyes of God.

During the recording of one of my messages titled "Honor Part 2", as I read from Ezekiel chapter 18, the Holy Spirit kept repeating the word "fruits." Now, I understand what He was trying to convey. Below is a simple explanation.

Ezekiel 18:5-9 tells us, "But if a man be just, and do that which is lawful and right, 6 And has not eaten upon the mountains (one fruit), neither has lifted up his eyes to the idols of the house of Israel (another fruit), neither has defiled his neighbor's wife (another fruit), neither has come near to a menstruous woman (another fruit), 7 And has not oppressed any, but has restored to the debtor his pledge (another fruit), has spoiled none by violence (another fruit), has given his bread to the hungry (another fruit), and has covered the naked with a garment (another fruit), 8 He that has not given forth upon usury, neither has taken any increase, that has withdrawn his hand from iniquity (all these are fruits), has executed true judgment between man and man (another fruit), 9 Has walked in my statutes and has kept my judgments, to deal truly (these are all fruits), he is just, he shall surely live, says the Lord God."

From this passage, we can see how the fruits of a child of God lead to eternal life.

My husband heard a story about a wealthy sister who used to assist a poor brother who had recently joined their church. Over time, the brother offended her and pleaded for forgiveness. Although she forgave him, she stopped providing the financial help she used to offer. Not long after, the sister passed away. Someone who wasn't even a church member but knew the sister had a dream. In the dream, the sister was dancing towards Heaven's gate but was halted by angels who informed her that they recognized her but needed to review the records.

Upon examining the books, they discovered that she had forgiven the brother but had withdrawn her support. Consequently, they directed her towards Hellfire. I pray that this will not be your fate in the name of Jesus. The brother who had the dream decided to travel to the sister's church, even though it was far away, to confirm the vision. Upon his arrival, everyone was saying that she had gone home to be with the Lord until the brother shared the dream, revealing that she did not make it to heaven. The congregation wept bitterly.

Ephesians 2:1-3 tells us, "And you He has quickened, who were dead in trespasses and sins; 2 Wherein in time past you walked according to the course of this world, according to the prince of the power of the air, the spirit that now works in the children of disobedience: 3 Among whom also we all had our conversation in times past in the lusts of our flesh, fulfilling the desires of the flesh and the mind, and were by nature the children of wrath, even as others."

This means that anyone who comes to Jesus goes from being dead in trespasses and sins to being alive in Christ Jesus and living for Him. They transition from walking according to the course of this world to walking according to the will of God, and from following the prince of the power of the air to following the leading of the Holy Spirit. Anyone who comes to Jesus moves from being a child of wrath on the path to hellfire to someone destined for Heaven whose name is written in the Lamb's Book of Life. There is a complete transformation in their walk and destination.

2 Corinthians 5:17 tells us, "Therefore, if any man be in Christ, he is a new creature: old things are passed away; behold, all things are become new."

John 1:12 tells us, "But as many as received Him, to them gave He power to become the sons of God, even to them that believe on His name: 13 Which were born, not of blood, nor of the will of the flesh, nor of the will of man, but of God."

When you receive Jesus into your life, you become someone born of God, empowered to be a son or daughter of God. God equips you with His power to face the challenges of sin, and you are never alone. You now have the power to say no to temptation, rebuke Satan, and call upon Jesus when you need Him.

I encourage you to give your life to this Jesus today. He is thoughtful, caring, and loving, and he will fully equip you to live the Christian life. He promised that He will never leave you or forsake you. He is your help in times of need, a friend closer than a brother or sister, and He will always be there for you.

This is the Jesus to whom I invite you to give your life today. He was crucified, buried, and risen. He is sitting in heavenly places at the right hand of the Father, far above all principality, power, might, dominion, and every name that is named, not only in this world but also in the world to come. If you give your life to Him, God will raise you with Him, causing you to sit in heavenly places in Him, and you will find no greater honor in this world. When the enemy tempts you, remind him that you are seated in heavenly places in Christ Jesus, and you will not let go of that privilege.

James 4:7 tells us, "Submit yourselves therefore to God. Resist the devil, and he will flee from you."

John 3:16-17 tells us, "For God so loved the world, that He gave His only begotten Son, that whosoever believes in Him should not perish but have everlasting life. 17 For God sent not His Son into the world to condemn the world, but that the world through Him might be saved."

It is time to say Jesus I repent please come into my life and save me. Then get baptized and follow him.

In conclusion, the profound analogy between a child of God created for good works and a fruit tree designed to bear fruit underscores the divine purpose inherent in every believer. Ephesians 2:8-10 emphasizes that salvation is a gift obtained through faith and not by works, but the subsequent call to walk in good works is not merely a commandment; it is the very purpose for which believers are created. Good works symbolized as the fruits of a Christian life, extend beyond benevolent actions and encapsulate a life aligned with God's commandments. The gravity of works is underscored in biblical passages warning against the consequences of barren trees and emphasizing the judgment based on deeds. The story of a sister's fate, as shared, serves as a poignant reminder that forgiveness alone may not suffice; it is the continuous bearing of good fruits that leads to eternal life.

The transformation brought about by coming to Jesus is a complete shift from a life of sin to a life lived following God's will. The invitation to embrace this transformative Jesus, who offers eternal life and empowers believers to overcome, stands as a compelling call to submit to God, resist the devil, and secure the promise of salvation through faith in Jesus Christ. As believers, we are called not only to receive grace but to manifest it through a life adorned with the fruits of righteousness, living out the purpose for which we were intricately designed in Christ Jesus.

2

Be Diligent!

The hour when Jesus will appear is approaching. Therefore, remain vigilant, be diligent, and overcome.

Revelation 3:1-6: "And unto the angel of the church in Sardis write; These things saith he that hath the seven Spirits of God, and the seven stars; I know thy works, that thou hast a name that thou livest, and art dead. 2 Be watchful, and strengthen the things which remain, that are ready to die: for I have not found thy works perfect before God 3 Remember therefore how thou hast received and heard, and hold fast, and repent. If therefore thou shalt not watch, I will come on thee as a thief, and thou shalt not know what hour I will come upon thee. 4 Thou hast a few names even in Sardis which have not defiled their garments; and they shall walk with me in white: for they are worthy. 5 He that overcometh, the same shall be clothed in white raiment; and I will not blot out his name out of the book of life, but I will confess his name before my Father, and before his angels. 6 He that hath an ear, let him hear what the Spirit saith unto the churches."

In the church of Sardis, only a few believers were found worthy to walk with Jesus in white raiment because they had not defiled themselves. The rest of the believers were not found worthy to walk with Jesus in white raiment because their works were not perfect in the eyes of God. Therefore, they were told to repent and watch, or else their names would be blotted out of the Book of Life.

To watch means that they will remain ready for the Return of Christ by keeping themselves in the light. If they overcome, their names will not be blotted out of the Book of Life. I pray that you will overcome in the name of Jesus Christ!

Galatians 5:19-21 tells us, "Now the works of the flesh are manifest, which are these; Adultery, fornication, uncleanness, lasciviousness 20 Idolatry, witchcraft, hatred, variance, emulations, wrath, strife, seditions, heresies, Envyings, murders, drunkenness, revellings, and such like: of the which I tell you before, as I have also told you in time past, that they which do such things shall not inherit the kingdom of God."

Imperfect works are the works of the flesh. Imperfect works are evil works. Imperfect works are not considered good works in the eyes of God. Imperfect works defile your spirit, but perfect works are works led by the Holy Spirit and do not defile a person.

Revelation 3:7-8 "And to the angel of the church in Philadelphia write; These things saith he that is holy, he that is true, he that hath the key of David, he that openeth, and no man shutteth; and shutteth, and no man openeth; 8 I know thy works: behold, I have set before thee an open door, and no man can shut it: for thou hast a little strength, and hast kept my word, and hast not denied my name."

Tribulation may weaken you, but the believers in the church of Philadelphia remained faithful to God's word during tribulation and did not deny His name and because of this, they were promised three honors – two in this world and one in eternity."

Honor Number One: Revelation 3:9 "Behold, I will make them of the synagogue of Satan, which say they are Jews, and are not, but do lie; behold, I will make them to come and worship before thy feet, and to know that I have loved thee."

Honor Number Two: Revelation 3:10 "Because thou hast kept the word of my patience, I also will keep thee from the hour of temptation, which shall come upon all the world, to try them that dwell upon the earth."

Honor Number Three: Revelation 3: 11-13 "Behold, I come quickly: hold that fast which thou hast, that no man take thy crown.12 Him that overcometh will I make a pillar in the temple of my God, and he shall go no more out: and I will write upon him the name of my God, and the name of the city of my God, which is new Jerusalem, which cometh down out of heaven from my God: and I will write upon him my new name.13 He that hath an ear, let him hear what the Spirit saith unto the churches."

The believers of the church of Philadelphia had little strength in this world, but in eternity, God would make them pillars in His temple, symbolizing strength. Why? Because they were wise and remained faithful to His word.

John 16: 33 "These things I have spoken unto you, that in me ye might have peace. In the world ye shall have tribulation: but be of good cheer; I have overcome the world."

If you are going through tribulation today, remember that Jesus has overcome the world, and you can too. Take courage and put your trust in Him.

2 Peter 3:10-14 says, "But the day of the Lord will come as a thief in the night; in the which the heavens shall pass away with a great noise, and the elements shall melt with fervent heat, the earth also and the works that are therein shall be burned up.11 Seeing then that all these things shall be dissolved, what manner of persons ought ye to be in all holy conversation and godliness,12 Looking for and hasting unto the coming of the day of God, wherein the heavens being on fire shall be dissolved, and the elements shall melt with fervent heat?13 Nevertheless we, according to his promise, look for new heavens and a new earth, wherein dwelleth righteousness.14 Wherefore, beloved, seeing that ye look for such things, be diligent that ye may be found of him in peace, without spot, and blameless."

In closing, let us heed the timeless wisdom found in Revelation, recognizing the call to diligence and vigilance in our faith. Just as the believers in Sardis were urged to strengthen their works and repent, and those in Philadelphia were promised honors for their faithfulness, we too are reminded to overcome the works of the flesh and remain stead-fast in God's word. As we face tribulations, let the assurance of Christ's victory encourage us to persevere. In anticipation of the day of the Lord, may we be found diligent, at peace, without spot, and blameless in His sight. May the Spirit's guidance lead us to overcome, just as we await the promised new heavens and a new earth. Be diligent, stand firm, and may the grace of our Lord Jesus Christ be with you all. Amen.

3

The Soul that Sinneth Shall Die

Fear the Lord with all your heart, for the soul that sins shall die.
Turn from evil to do what's right. Come back to Jesus.
Walk in the light.

Ezekiel 18:4 tells us, "The soul that sinneth shall die." Let me provide an example of this. The destruction of the cities of Sodom and Gomorrah in Genesis 19 serves as an illustration of "the soul that sinneth shall die."

Sodom and Gomorrah were cities in the Bible where the people practiced abominations in the eyes of God. Tired of their prolonged involvement in homosexuality and ungodliness, God rained fire and brimstone upon them, destroying everyone except Lot and his family because "the soul that sinneth shall die."

Many people claim to know Jesus but are homosexuals and lesbians. God is warning you to come out of this because "the soul that sinneth shall die." Cry out to God for deliverance until you receive it. Let God see that you acknowledge that homosexuality is wrong because homosexuals will not inherit eternal life. Do not deceive yourself; the Bible states that no unclean thing will enter Heaven. God is holy, and

He demands holiness from His children. Therefore, repent and return to Jesus.

There is no doubt about it. A sinning soul will eventually perish in hellfire. Sin destroys souls and leads them to hell, but turning away from sin can save a soul.

The Wicked

Ezekiel 18:20-22 tells us,
"The soul that sinneth, it shall die. The son shall not bear the iniquity of the father, neither shall the father bear the iniquity of the son: the righteousness of the righteous shall be upon him, and the wickedness of the wicked shall be upon him. But if the wicked turns from all his sins that he has committed, and keeps all my statutes, and does what is lawful and right, he shall surely live; he shall not die. All his transgressions that he has committed shall not be mentioned unto him: in his righteousness that he has done, he shall live."

Do you desire to inherit eternal life? Then repent, give your life to Jesus, be baptized, and obey Him. Do you wish to live forever after death? Then repent, give your life to Jesus, be baptized, and obey Him because "the soul that sinneth shall die."

Ezekiel 18:27 tells us,
"Again, when the wicked man turns away from his wickedness that he has committed, and does what is lawful and right, he shall save his soul alive."

A soul is saved by repenting, turning away from wickedness to Jesus, and doing what is lawful and right in the eyes of the Lord.

The Righteous

Ezekiel 18:24 tells us,

"But when the righteous turns away from his righteousness, and commits iniquity, and does according to all the abominations that the wicked man does, shall he live? All his righteousness that he has done shall not be mentioned: in his trespass that he has trespassed, and in his sin that he has sinned, in them shall he die. When a righteous man turns away from his righteousness, and commits iniquity, and dies in them; for his iniquity that he has done shall he die."

A soul perishes and goes to hell when a righteous person turns from righteousness to commit iniquity and dies without repenting. This chapter tells us that all the good they have done will be forgotten and remembered no more.

The good news is that God takes no pleasure in the wicked perishing and going to hell (Ezekiel 18:23). He desires all to be saved. You can be saved by repenting and returning to Jesus.

I John 1:9 If we confess our sins, he is faithful and just to forgive us our sins, and to cleanse us from all unrighteousness.

In conclusion, the solemn warning echoes through the ages: "The soul that sinneth shall die." The account of Sodom and Gomorrah stands as a stark reminder of the consequences of unrepentant sin, illustrating that God's judgment is inevitable for those who persist in wickedness.

Yet, there is hope and mercy in this sobering truth. The passage from Ezekiel emphasizes the individual responsibility for one's actions, affirming that righteousness brings life, while sin leads to death. It is a call to turn away from wickedness, to embrace the light of Jesus, and to walk in the path of righteousness.

To those entangled in lifestyles contrary to God's design, the plea is clear: repent and return to Jesus. The God who desires not the death of the wicked, but their salvation beckons with open arms. Acknowledge the truth, seek deliverance, and let the transformative power of Christ guide you into righteousness.

For the righteous, the caution is not to grow complacent. The righteous can fall, and their past goodness will not shield them if they turn away from righteousness. The urgency to remain steadfast in faith and obedience resonates through the scriptures, reminding us that a righteous soul can perish through unrepentant iniquity.

In the grand narrative of salvation, God's mercy shines brightly. He delights in the repentance of the wicked and longs for all to be saved. The key lies in turning away from sin, embracing righteousness, and, above all, returning to Jesus. In doing so, one can find the assurance of salvation and the promise of eternal life.

May this closing statement serve as a clarion call to all souls, urging them to heed the warnings, embrace the grace offered by Jesus, and secure the hope of life everlasting.

4

Witnesses that Jesus is the Son of God

Eternal life is found in no other son but the Son of God.

The Witness of God

In 1 John 5:9-13, we are reminded that the testimony of God is of greater significance than that of men. The passage asserts that those who believe in the Son of God have this testimony within themselves, while those who do not believe make God out to be a liar by rejecting His account of His Son. The record is clear: God has granted eternal life through His Son, and possessing the Son means possessing life. The purpose of these words is to reassure believers that they possess eternal life and to encourage continued faith in the Son of God.

"Why should I believe that Jesus is the Son of God?" you may ask. The answer lies in the divine record that God has provided about His Son. God, the ultimate witness in this passage, affirms that Jesus is the Son of God and has been endowed with eternal life. The testimony of God holds greater weight than that of men.

Consider the analogy of a mother's intimate knowledge of the gifts she bestows upon her children. Similarly, God has revealed that He has granted eternal life to His Son, Jesus. We, as witnesses, can affirm and testify to this divine revelation.

The Witness of Men

John 20:31 serves as a purpose statement for the entire chapter, emphasizing that its contents are crafted to persuade belief in Jesus as the Christ, the Son of God. The chapter presents compelling evidence, including Mary Magdalene's discovery of the empty tomb, Peter and another disciple's observation of Jesus's clothes and the napkin, and Jesus's appearances to the disciples, all contributing to their belief.

Notably, Thomas initially doubted the disciples' account until he witnessed the wounds on Jesus's hands and side. Jesus's response, recorded in verse 29, underscores the blessedness of those who believe without seeing. The chapter aims to convince readers to believe in the Son of God.

Acts 10:37-43 recounts the testimony of men who were witnesses to Jesus's ministry, crucifixion, and resurrection. This passage highlights the proclamation of salvation through faith in Jesus and echoes the words of the prophets, emphasizing that through His name, believers receive forgiveness of sins.

In summary, the passage emphasizes the divine witness to Jesus as the Son of God, stressing that eternal life is found only through belief in Him. The testimony of God, as presented in 1 John 5:9-13, asserts that those who believe in the Son of God possess the witness within themselves. The narrative further illustrates the witness of men in John 20, using events like the empty tomb, appearances to disciples, and the skepticism of Thomas. The purpose of John 20 is to convince readers that Jesus is the Christ, the Son of God. Acts 10:37-43 reinforces this conviction, detailing the witness of those who saw Jesus after His resurrection and proclaiming the salvation available through belief in His name. The call to believe is extended, urging readers to accept this testimony and embrace faith in Jesus Christ.

5

The Judgment Seat of Christ

Strive to be accepted by Jesus. Do not sleep, slumber, or be slothful.

Just as there are judges on earth, there is also a Judge in Heaven before whom we will all stand one day. While He is normally portrayed as a God of love – and He is – in the book of 2 Corinthians 5, the Apostle Paul talks about His terror, stating that this is the reason why he "persuades men."

2 Corinthians 5:8-9 tells us, "We are confident, I say, and willing rather to be absent from the body and to be present with the Lord. 9 Wherefore we labor, that whether present or absent, we may be accepted of Him."

Did the Apostle Paul just say that we must labor to be accepted by God, whether we are present or absent from the body? Moreover, it's intriguing that when most preachers and teachers paraphrase verse 8, it is rarely used along with verse 9, which is of utmost importance. It is often employed to create peace of mind rather than to provide a warning.

2 Corinthians 5:10-11 tells us, "For we must all appear before the judgment seat of Christ, that everyone may receive the things done in

his body, according to that he hath done, whether it be good or bad. 11 Knowing, therefore, the terror of the Lord, we persuade men."

To be absent from the body should be a matter of concern for all believers, not something to rejoice about, as we do not know if we will be accepted or rejected at the judgment seat of Christ.

Therefore, I urge you to come out of the club of the do-nothings and make it into heaven believers. Come out of the club of those who believe they can do as much evil as they please and still make it into heaven. Come out of the club of those who think there is more than one way to get to heaven because Jesus is the only way!

Come out of the club of people who adhere to such teachings and instead labor to be accepted by God, for "strait is the gate, and narrow is the way, which leadeth unto life, and few there be that find it. But broad is the way, that leadeth to destruction, and many there be which go in thereat" (Matthew 7:13-14).

Here is an example of what the Apostle Paul was speaking about in 2 Corinthians 5:10-11 concerning the Judgment Seat of Christ.

Matthew 25:31-41 "When the Son of man shall come in his glory, and all the holy angels with him, then shall he sit upon the throne of his glory: 32 And before him shall be gathered all nations: and he shall separate them one from another, as a shepherd divideth his sheep from the goats: 33 And he shall set the sheep on his right hand, but the goats on the left. 34 Then shall the King say unto them on his right hand, Come, ye blessed of my Father, inherit the kingdom prepared for you from the foundation of the world: 35 For I was an hungred, and ye gave me meat: I was thirsty, and ye gave me drink: I was a stranger, and ye took me in: 36 Naked, and ye clothed me: I was sick, and ye visited me: I was in prison, and ye came unto me. 37 Then shall the righteous answer him, saying, Lord, when saw we thee an hungred, and fed thee? or thirsty, and gave thee drink? 38 When saw we thee a stranger, and took thee in? or naked, and clothed thee? 39 Or when saw we thee sick, or in prison, and came unto thee? 40 And the King shall answer and say unto them, Verily I say unto you, Inasmuch as ye have done it unto one of the least of these my brethren, ye have done it unto me. 41 Then shall he say also unto them on the left hand, Depart from me, ye cursed, into everlasting fire, prepared for the devil and his angels: 42 For I was an hungred, and ye gave me no meat: I was thirsty, and ye gave me no drink: 43 I was a stranger, and ye took me not in: naked, and ye clothed me not: sick, and in prison, and ye visited me not. 44 Then shall they also answer him, saying, Lord, when saw we thee an hungred, or athirst, or a stranger, or naked, or sick, or in prison, and did not minister unto thee? 45 Then shall he answer them, saying, Verily I say unto you, Inasmuch as ye did it not to one of the least of these, ye did it not to me. 46 And these shall go away into everlasting punishment: but the righteous into life eternal."

In conclusion, let these words echo as a solemn reminder of the gravity of our choices and the impending reality of standing before the Judgment Seat of Christ. The urgency to labor for acceptance by the Lord, as emphasized by the Apostle Paul, resounds in our hearts. As we navigate our earthly journey, let us not be lulled into complacency or misled by false assurances. The parable in Matthew 25 vividly illustrates the criteria by which we will be judged – not by empty professions, but by our tangible expressions of love and compassion towards others. May we heed this call to come out of the shadows of indifference and self-deception, striving to follow the narrow path that leads to life eternal. My prayer is that these words serve as a catalyst for self-reflection, genuine repentance, and a fervent pursuit of a life worthy of acceptance at the Judgment Seat of Christ. May the grace of the Lord guide our steps, revealing the way to eternal glory. Amen.

6

Great Things He Has Done

Weep no more because this time you will catch something beyond your wildest dreams!

Psalm 30:1-3 declares, "I will extol thee, O Lord; for thou hast lifted me up, and hast not made my foes to rejoice over me. 2 O Lord my God, I cried unto thee, and thou hast healed me. 3 O Lord, thou hast brought up my soul from the grave: thou hast kept me alive, that I should not go down to the pit."

There was a time when King Saul pursued David relentlessly, seeking to take his life because of the glory upon him. The situation escalated to the point where David had to flee to another country to escape Saul's threats. However, in due time, King Saul passed away, and David ascended to the throne in all his glory, experiencing the peace that God granted him from all his adversaries.

Therefore, I prophesy that the Saul in your life will soon be cut off in the name of Jesus.

I prophesy that you are entering a season of peace, free from the grip of all your enemies.

I prophesy that you will be elevated to the throne of your glory.

I prophesy that your weeping will transform into joy.

I prophesy that your mourning will turn into dancing, and you will exalt the Lord God for the remarkable things He has done for you.

John 21:3-6 recounts, "Simon Peter saith unto them, I go a fishing. They say unto him, We also go with thee. They went forth, and entered into a ship immediately; and that night they caught nothing. 4 But when the morning was now come, Jesus stood on the shore: but the disciples knew not that it was Jesus. 5 Then Jesus saith unto them, Children, have ye any meat? They answered him, No. 6 And he said unto them, Cast the net on the right side of the ship, and ye shall find. They cast therefore, and now they were not able to draw it for the multitude of fishes."

To whoever is listening, abundance is on its way! You may have been toiling all night without results, but this time, you will catch something beyond your wildest imagination, declares the Spirit of the Lord!

Weeping may endure for a night, but joy comes in the morning. Your morning has arrived. Shout Hallelujah!

7

The Unveiling of the Mystery

If God can send a Jew to a Gentile, then God can send anyone
to any nation.

In Ephesians 3:1-9, the Apostle Paul speaks to us about a mystery revealed to him by divine revelation. So, what is this mystery? It can be found in Ephesians 3:6, which states, "That the Gentiles should be fellow heirs, and of the same body, and partakers of His promise in Christ by the gospel."

Who are the Gentiles? Simply put, they are not Jews. According to the Apostle Paul, a Jew sent to preach the gospel to the Gentiles, there is no superiority of Jews over Gentile Christians. All are equal partakers in the promise of the gospel, saved by grace through faith, and recipients of the gift of the Holy Spirit. Eternal life is bestowed upon all without discrimination. God uses them all according to His will, and belief in the Lord Jesus is the key. The gospel is not exclusive to the Jews.

Matthew 12:17 tells us, "That it might be fulfilled which was spoken by Isaiah the prophet, saying, 'Behold my servant, whom I have chosen; my beloved, in whom my soul is well pleased: I will put my spirit upon him, and he shall show judgment to the Gentiles...'" This prophecy refers to Jesus.

Isaiah foresaw that the Gentiles would put their trust in Jesus, and this prophecy has come to pass. For example, I am not a Jew, yet I have put my trust in Jesus, as have many others who are not Jews.

Acts 11:13-18 recounts the story of Cornelius, a Gentile, and Peter, a Jew. Peter, realizing that the Holy Spirit had been given to the Gentiles as it had been to the Jews, acknowledges that he cannot oppose what God has done for the Gentiles. He emphasizes that God has granted repentance unto life for the Gentiles.

Mark 3:31-35 narrates an incident where Jesus emphasizes that true kinship in the kingdom of God is not determined by one's Jewish or Gentile identity but by doing the will of God. Those who do God's will are considered Jesus' true family. They are the true mothers, and sisters, and brothers of Jesus.

Romans 6:23 states, "For the wages of sin is death, but the gift of God is eternal life through Jesus Christ our Lord."

In conclusion, the unveiling of the mystery in Ephesians illuminates a divine plan that transcends cultural boundaries and shatters the barriers between Jew and Gentile.

The narrative of Cornelius and Peter in Acts, coupled with the prophetic words of Isaiah, vividly illustrates the fulfillment of God's promise to the Gentiles. As we navigate the passages of Matthew and Mark, we witness Jesus' emphasis on a universal kinship based not on heritage but on obedience to the will of God.

Paul's teachings reinforce the idea that salvation, the gift of the Holy Spirit, and eternal life are extended impartially to all who believe in the Lord Jesus. The resounding truth echoing through these scriptures is that in the kingdom of God, distinctions fade, and unity prevails. Thus, our response is not rooted in our heritage but in our shared commitment to the will of God.

Romans 6:23 encapsulates the essence of this universal gospel – the wages of sin may be death, but through Jesus Christ, God extends the eternal gift of life to all who believe. As we embrace this truth, we become not only heirs of a divine promise but also ambassadors of a message that invites all, irrespective of their background, to partake in the richness of God's grace.

Conquering Fear and Activating God-Given Gifts

Embrace the journey of destiny; let the restoration of your mind silence the whispers of fear along the way.

Fear is a common human emotion, but as mentioned in 2 Timothy 1:6-7, the power of the Holy Spirit can help us overcome it: "For God hath not given us the spirit of fear; but of power, and of love, and of a sound mind."

This passage reminds us that fear is not from God, and through the Holy Spirit, we can find the strength, love, and sound judgment needed to confront and conquer our fears.

Fear used to limit me when I sang at one point, but one day the Lord assured me that He would anoint me in such a way that fear would no longer be a constraint. Today, as I open my mouth to sing, I am astounded by the transformative power infused into my voice. This experience is a testament to what God can do through His Holy Spirit.

The release from fear and the newfound strength in my singing serve as a reminder of the remarkable ways in which God empowers and transforms those who trust in Him.

To utilize the gifts and talents God has given us, it's essential to stir up these gifts, as suggested in 2 Timothy 1:6.

Whether you have the gift of singing, teaching, or preaching, using these gifts is a way to grow and fulfill your purpose. In essence, it means actively and passionately using your God-given abilities.

In times of adversity and fear, as seen in Acts 4:31, we can turn to God in prayer for boldness. The Holy Spirit can fill us with courage and help us continue to spread His word and do His work, even in the face of challenges.

Acts 1:8 emphasizes the transformative power of the Holy Spirit. When the Holy Spirit comes upon us, it equips us with the power to be a witness for Christ and carry out the tasks we are called to do. Therefore, seeking the Holy Spirit is a vital aspect of our spiritual journey.

When fear creeps into our hearts, as expressed in Psalm 56:3, we can turn to God for refuge and place our trust in Him.

Trusting in God and remembering that He has not given us a spirit of fear can help us find peace and courage during our fears.

May your trust in God help you overcome your fears, and may you be liberated from the spirit of fear through the empowering presence of the Holy Spirit. In Jesus' name, amen.

9

Offer the Sacrifices of Righteousness

Choose to meditate on the word of God and offer the sacrifices of righteousness, for in doing so, we walk a path illuminated by the glory of His faithfulness.

Psalm 4:5 encourages us to "offer the sacrifices of righteousness and put our trust in the Lord." This verse reminds us of the importance of maintaining our integrity and trust in God, even when faced with temptations or challenges.

A powerful illustration of this principle is when I had the opportunity to obtain a cell phone through dishonest means but chose to trust in God's provision instead. In doing so, I not only maintained my integrity but was also pleasantly surprised by God's faithfulness when He provided me with a better cell phone. This serves as a valuable lesson in the wisdom of putting our trust in the Lord, knowing that He will supply our needs according to His riches in glory.

An example of offering the sacrifices of righteousness can be found in Luke 9:23, which tells us to deny ourselves, take up our cross daily, and follow Jesus. To deny oneself means turning away from wrongdoing and embracing what is right, leaving behind the old life to pursue a new life in Christ. It requires making the conscious choice to follow Jesus, even in times of suffering, pain, and hardship.

Psalm 119:97 tells us, "Oh, how I love your law! It is my meditation all the day." Meditation on the word of God is another way to offer the sacrifices of righteousness. Delighting yourself in the law of the Lord is another way of offering the sacrifices of righteousness as well as loving it. All these represent offering the sacrifices of righteousness to the Lord.

Instead of joking all day, choose to meditate on the word of God. Instead of watching TV, TikTok videos, or ungodly shows all day, choose to offer the sacrifices of righteousness instead by meditating on the word of the Lord. Instead of dwelling on negative thoughts that make you angry, humble yourself and let God take care of it. Instead of meditating on things that lack praise or virtue, offer the sacrifices of righteousness, and meditate on the word of God so you can grow and bring forth your fruits in your season. In addition to this, take what you read in the word of God and turn it into prayers.

May the Lord's blessings and protection be with you as you continue to walk in righteousness and trust in Him, in the mighty name of Jesus. Amen.

10

Diligently Seek God

Diligently seek God with all your heart, and allow His glory
and honor to overflow upon you.

Hebrews 11:5 tells us, "By faith Enoch was translated that he should not see death; and was not found, because God had translated him: for before his translation he had this testimony, that he pleased God."

If God had to give a testimony of you today, what do you think that he would say? Will he label you as a rapist? A liar? A hater? A murderer? A thief or an adulterous woman? Or will he call you a vessel of honor, a virtuous woman who pleases Him? Enoch entered heaven because he pleased God. Are you currently pleasing God? If God were to give His testimony about you today, what would He say?

Hebrews 11:6 states, "But without faith, it is impossible to please him: for he that cometh to God must believe that he is and that he is a rewarder of them that diligently seek him."

It takes faith to come to God and to walk with Him. No one can approach God without first believing that He exists, is real, and that He is the Almighty God, a Rewarder for those who earnestly seek Him. How do you come to God? You come to God through His Son, Jesus.

Enoch reached Heaven because he diligently sought God. He wasn't a Christian today and something else tomorrow, or a Christian for six months and then not for another six months. He wasn't a Christian who walked with God until he was ready to mistreat his neighbor and rob them. Enoch diligently sought God, living in a way that recognized the uncertainty of the day when the trumpet will sound, and Jesus will return. Therefore, I urge you to diligently seek God today.

Matthew 6:25-33 advises, "Therefore I say unto you, Take no thought for your life, what ye shall eat, or what ye shall drink; nor yet for your body, what ye shall put on. Is not the life more than meat, and the body than raiment? 26 Behold the fowls of the air: for they sow not, neither do they reap, nor gather into barns; yet your heavenly Father feedeth them. Are ye not much better than they? 27 Which of you by taking thought can add one cubit unto his stature? 28 And why take ye thought for raiment? Consider the lilies of the field, how they grow; they toil not, neither do they spin: 29 And yet I say unto you, that even Solomon in all his glory was not arrayed like one of these. 30 Wherefore, if God so clothe the grass of the field, which today is, and tomorrow is cast into the oven, shall he not much more clothe you, O ye of little faith? 31 Therefore take no thought, saying, what shall we eat? or, what shall we drink? or, Wherewithal shall we be clothed? 32 (For after all these things do the Gentiles seek:) for your heavenly Father knoweth that ye have need of all these things. 33 But seek ye first the kingdom of God, and his righteousness; and all these things shall be added unto you."

To diligently seek God is to prioritize seeking the kingdom of God first and His righteousness. God promises that all your needs will be provided because He is a Rewarder for those who diligently seek Him, not only in this life but also in the life to come.

Honor in Eternity

In your deeds, you script your destiny in the kingdom of God. Therefore, depart from evil and choose honor today.

One day, Jesus will return to ask you to give an account of the goods that He delivered into your hands, and depending on what you did with His resources, you will either be honored or dishonored.

Matthew 25:14-30 tells us that the kingdom of Heaven is like a man traveling into a far country, who called his own servants and delivered to them his goods. To one, he gave five talents, to another two talents, and to another one talent according to their abilities. Then he went on his way.

While he was away, the servant who received five talents gained another five talents. The servant who received two talents gained another two talents, but the servant who was given one talent gained nothing because he buried his Lord's money in the earth. Due to this, he was cast into outer darkness or hellfire.

The ones who doubled their money received the honor from their master, who said to them, "Well done, my good and faithful servant, you have been faithful over a few things, I will make you ruler over many things; enter into the joy of the Lord."

What you do with God's money will determine whether you will inherit eternal life or be condemned to hellfire. Your faithfulness to the resources God has entrusted you with will lead you to honor, while unfaithfulness will lead to dishonor. Your faithfulness to the resources that God has committed into your hands will lead you into the joy of the Lord, but unfaithfulness will lead you to weeping and gnashing of teeth. The choice is yours.

The Apostle Paul said to Timothy in I Timothy 4:16, "Take heed unto thyself and unto the doctrine: continue in them: for in doing this thou shalt both save thyself, and them that hear thee."

God has given us social media platforms on which to teach, and whatever is posted should reflect sound doctrine. Otherwise, it may lead to hellfire for both the speaker and the listeners. When Jesus returns, He will honor all those who taught sound doctrine and continued in it. Those who did the opposite will be dishonored, and there will be wailing and gnashing of teeth.

Matthew 25:31-34 tells us, "When the Son of man shall come in His glory, and all the holy angels with Him, then shall He sit upon the throne of His glory: And before Him shall be gathered all nations: and He shall separate them one from another, as a shepherd divideth his sheep from the goats: And He shall set the sheep on His right hand, but the goats on the left. Then shall the King say unto them on His right hand, Come, ye blessed of My Father, inherit the kingdom prepared for you from the foundation of the world."

This is the reason for their honor. Matthew 25:35-40, "For I was an hungred, and ye gave me meat: I was thirsty, and ye gave me drink: I was a stranger, and ye took me in: 36 Naked, and ye clothed me: I was sick, and ye visited me: I was in prison, and ye came unto me. 37 Then shall the righteous answer him, saying, Lord, when saw we thee an hungred, and fed thee? or thirsty, and gave thee drink? 38 When saw we thee a stranger, and took thee in? or naked, and clothed thee? 39 Or when saw we thee sick, or in prison, and came unto thee? 40 And the King shall answer and say unto them, Verily I say unto you, Inasmuch as ye have done it unto one of the least of these my brethren, ye have done it unto me."

Conversely, evil deeds and not ministering to the saints will lead to dishonor.

Matthew 25:41-46 "Then shall he say also unto them on the left hand, Depart from me, ye cursed, into everlasting fire, prepared for the devil and his angels: 42 For I was an hungred, and ye gave me no meat: I was thirsty, and ye gave me no drink: 43 I was a stranger, and ye took me not in: naked, and ye clothed me not: sick, and in prison, and ye visited me not. 44 Then shall they also answer him, saying, Lord, when saw we thee an hungred, or athirst, or a stranger, or naked, or sick, or in prison, and did not minister unto thee? 45 Then shall he answer them, saying, Verily I say unto you, Inasmuch as ye did it not to one of the least of these, ye did it not to me. 46 And these shall go away into everlasting punishment: but the righteous into life eternal."

Acts 26:14 "And when we were all fallen to the earth, I heard a voice speaking unto me, and saying in the Hebrew tongue, Saul, Saul, why persecutest thou me? it is hard for thee to kick against the pricks."

This verse explains to us what happens to people who persecute Christians. They are going to hurt themselves eventually if they do not repent. Fortunately for Saul, he repented and escaped the judgment of God.

No one who bullies a child of God will inherit eternal life. Swindling a child of God will not lead to eternal life. Only those who do good to a child of God will inherit eternal life unless they repent and return to Jesus.

Hebrews 6:10 reassures, "For God is not unrighteous to forget your work and labor of love, which ye have showed toward His name, in that ye have ministered to the saints, and do minister."

Again, this Bible verse is telling us that those who minister to the saints will inherit eternal life, while those who do not, will not inherit eternal life.

As we navigate the journey of life, let us bear in mind the profound truth that our choices echo in eternity. Each act of faithfulness, every instance of ministering to the saints, and the fidelity to sound doctrine carve the script of our destiny in the kingdom of God. The parable in Matthew 25 underscores the gravity of our decisions, pointing toward the ultimate contrast of honor and dishonor. Let us, therefore, approach each opportunity, each talent, with the gravity of eternal implications. May our lives resonate with the call to diligently seek God, for in our commitment to His will, we secure not just earthly success but an everlasting honor in the joy of the Lord.

12

Honor in Eternity II

In eternity, honor awaits the righteous; choose repentance,
and bear fruits for eternal destiny.

Discovering the wisdom in Ezekiel's teachings, this article explores the timeless choice between honor and dishonor in eternity. Examining the impact of righteousness and repentance versus straying from God's path, emphasizes the call to renew and produce meaningful fruits. Join this journey to understand the vital role of choices in shaping eternal destinies and embracing a regenerated life of honor in God's eyes.

Ezekiel 18:5-9 tells us, "But if a man be just and does what is lawful and right—having not eaten upon the mountains, neither lifted up his eyes to the idols of the house of Israel, neither defiled his neighbor's wife, neither come near to a menstruous woman, neither oppressed any, but restored to the debtor his pledge, spoiled none by violence, given his bread to the hungry, and covered the naked with a garment; he that has not given forth upon usury, neither taken any increase, that has withdrawn his hand from iniquity, executed true judgment between man and man, walked in God's statutes, and kept His judgments to deal truly—he is just; he shall surely live," says the Lord God. But, "The soul that sinneth it shall die," Ezekiel 18:2, which means that this soul will not inherit eternal life.

Psalm 51:10 tells us, "Create in me a clean heart, O God; and renew a right spirit within me."

When David departed from the way of righteousness to the way of wickedness, he prayed a prayer that included these words to renew him because sin makes everything unclean—your mind, your heart, and your spirit. And your spirit, born of God, perfect, holy, and right, becomes unclean and needs to be renewed.

Ezekiel 18:21 tells us, "But if the wicked will turn from all his sins that he has committed, and keep all my statutes, and do what is lawful and right, he shall surely live; he shall not die. All his transgressions that he has committed shall not be mentioned unto him; in his righteousness that he has done, he shall live."

King David turned from his sins and he lived and inherited eternal life, and it is going to be the same for all who will turn from their sins. They will live and inherit eternal life.

Ezekiel 18:24 tells us, "But when the righteous turns away from his righteousness and commits iniquity, and does according to all the abominations that the wicked man does, shall he live? All his righteousness that he has done shall not be mentioned; in his trespass that he has trespassed, and in his sin that he has sinned, in them shall he die."

When King David turned away from righteousness to wickedness, he was on his way to death and hellfire, and it is the same for any righteous person who turns away from righteousness to do the works of wickedness. They will be on their way to death and hellfire because the soul that sinneth shall die.

Therefore, if you know that you have turned from doing the works of righteousness to doing the works of wickedness, the trumpet is sounding once again for you: repent and come back to Jesus because there is no honor for the soul that dies in sin in eternity.

The fruits you bring forth will determine where you will spend eternity.

When John the Baptist saw the Pharisees and Sadducees coming for baptism, he said to them, "Bring forth therefore fruits meet for repentance: And think not to say within yourselves, we have Abraham to our father: for I say unto you, that God is able of these stones to raise up children unto Abraham. And now also the axe is laid unto the root of the trees; therefore, every tree which brings not forth good fruit is hewn down and cast into the fire," Matthew 3:8-10.

Fornicators will not inherit eternal life. Adulterers will not inherit eternal life. Thieves will not inherit eternal life. Witches will not inherit eternal life. Murderers will not inherit eternal life. Idolaters will not inherit eternal life. People who hire agents of darkness against children of God, burn candles against children of God, and invoke demons against children of God will not inherit eternal life, but those who bring forth the fruits meet for repentance are the ones who will be honored and inherit eternal life when Jesus returns.

The message of "do nothing and get to Heaven" is a hellfire message, and it will lead those who teach it to hellfire as well as those who hear it. When Jesus returns, he will be coming back to destroy the wicked husbandmen who did not render to him the fruits of the kingdom.

Matthew 21:43 tells us, "Therefore say I unto you, the kingdom of God shall be taken from you, and given to a nation bringing forth the fruits thereof."

There is honor, happiness, joy, and peace waiting for all those who bring forth the fruits of the kingdom, but there is dishonor for wicked servants who did not produce the fruits of the kingdom. There is going to be weeping and gnashing of teeth.

Matthew 24:37-41 tells us, "But as the days of Noah were, so shall also the coming of the Son of man be. For as in the days that were before the flood, they were eating and drinking, marrying and giving in marriage until the day that Noah entered into the ark, and knew not until the flood came and took them all away; so shall also the coming of the Son of man be. Then shall two be in the field; the one shall be taken, and the other left. Two women shall be grinding at the mill; the one shall be taken, and the other left."

My prayer for you is that you will not be the one who was left behind.

Matthew 24:42-51 tells us, "Watch therefore: for ye know not what hour your Lord doth come. But know this, that if the goodman of the house had known in what watch the thief would come, he would have watched and would not have suffered his house to be broken up. Therefore, be ye also ready: for in such an hour as ye think not, the Son of man cometh. Who then is a faithful and wise servant, whom his lord hath made ruler over his household, to give them meat in due season? Blessed is that servant, whom his lord when he cometh shall find so doing. Verily I say unto you, That he shall make him ruler over all his goods. But and if that evil servant shall say in his heart, My lord delayeth his coming; and shall begin to smite his fellowservants, and to eat and drink with the drunken; (swindle the poor, run ploys, run schemes, and bully the children of God.) The lord of that servant shall come in a day when he looketh not for him, and in an hour that he is not aware of, and shall cut him asunder, and appoint him his portion with the hypocrites: there shall be weeping and gnashing of teeth."

My prayer for you is that you will not be found a hypocrite when Jesus returns or when you die.

In conclusion, the scriptures underscore the profound impact of our choices on our eternal destiny. The path of righteousness, marked by repentance and the production of fruits meet for repentance, leads to honor and the promise of eternal life. Conversely, turning away from righteousness invites spiritual death. The urgency to heed the trumpet's call for repentance is clear—there is no honor for a soul that persists in sin. As we navigate this journey, the call to produce meaningful fruits aligns with the teachings of Matthew 3:8-10, emphasizing the necessity of genuine transformation. The analogy of Christ's return in Matthew 24 urges vigilance, and the hope offered in John 3:16 beckons us to embrace faith in Jesus for the assurance of eternal life. May this message resonate as both a warning and an invitation, guiding us toward a life worthy of honor in eternity.

13

Embracing Jesus: The Divine Creator and Sustainer of Life

Believe in Jesus, the Creator of worlds and the Savior of souls,
whose words bring forth life and light in us.

Hebrews 1:1-2 tells us, "God, who at sundry times and in divers manners spoke in time past unto the fathers by the prophets, 2 has in these last days spoken unto us by his Son, whom he has appointed heir of all things, by whom also he made the worlds."

If you did not know it, the worlds were made by Jesus.

Colossians 1:15-16 tells us, "Who is the image of the invisible God, the firstborn of every creature: 16 For by him were all things created, that are in heaven, and that are on earth, visible and invisible, whether they be thrones, or dominions, or principalities, or powers: all things were created by him, and for him: 17 And he is before all things, and by him all things consist."

Jesus made nothing with tools, machinery, or building plans, but everything he created was made by the word of God. He spoke it and it appeared. He declared it and it was so except when he created man.

He said, "Let there be light," and light appeared.

He said, "Let there be a firmament in the midst of the waters, and let it divide the waters from the waters," and the heaven was made.

He said, let the waters under the heaven be gathered into one place," and the Seas were made. He said, "Let the dry land appear," and the Earth was made.

He said, "Let there be lights in the firmament of the heaven to divide the day from the night," and the sun, the moon, and the stars were made.

He said, "Let the waters bring forth abundantly the moving creature that has life, and fowl that may fly above the earth," and the whales, the fishes, the turtles, the birds, and sea animals.

He said, "Let the earth bring forth the living creature after his kind, cattle, and creeping thing, and beast of the earth after his kind," and the cows, and the bugs, and the lions, and the elephants, and the bears and so on were made.

All these things were created by Jesus through His words, and He is still making things happen today through his words.

One day I had to share the word of God, and when I went up to the pulpit, the Lord said to me, "Preach Teach." Then I said to the Lord, "Lord, I know how to teach but I do not know how to preach," and to my surprise, I preached and taught that day, and that was not the last time I heard the voice of the Lord speaking things into my life that manifested. Jesus still has the power to speak and make things appear.

Hebrews 1:1-2 tells us, "God, who at sundry times and in divers manners spoke in time past unto the fathers by the prophets, 2 has in these last days spoken unto us by his Son."

Here are some things that God spoke to us by his Son Jesus after he was risen.

Mark 16:15-18 tells us, "And he said unto them, Go ye into all the world, and preach the gospel to every creature. 16 He that believeth and is baptized shall be saved; but he that believeth not shall be damned. 17 And these signs shall follow them that believe; In my name shall they cast out devils; they shall speak with new tongues; 18 They shall take up serpents; and if they drink any deadly thing, it shall not hurt them; they shall lay hands on the sick, and they shall recover."

One day I was on the streets doing the work of God when I met a woman who told me that she used to be a Christian but now she serves Buddha. I thought to myself what a wrong step to take; then I laid my hands on her and prayed for her restoration.

Hebrews 3:12-14 tells us, "Take heed, brethren, lest there be in any of you an evil heart of unbelief, in departing from the living God. 13 But exhort one another daily, while it is called Today; lest any of you be hardened through the deceitfulness of sin. 14 For we are made partakers of Christ if we hold the beginning of our confidence steadfast unto the end."

You cannot inherit the promise if you do not continue to believe in Jesus. The woman I met on the street once believed, but at some point, she no longer believed, and there are many like her today who have been hardened by the deceitfulness of sin and no longer believe in Jesus.

Hebrews 3:15-19 tells us, while it is said, "Today if ye will hear his voice, harden not your hearts, as in the provocation. 16 For some, when they had heard, did provoke: howbeit not all that came out of Egypt by Moses. 17 But with whom was he grieved forty years? was it not with them that had sinned, whose carcasses fell in the wilderness? 18 And to whom sware he that they should not enter into his rest, but to them that believed not? 19 So we see that they could not enter in because of unbelief."

This woman departed from Jesus because she did not believe in him anymore. Will her name still be written in the Lamb's Book of Life when she is following someone else? Anyone who leaves a marriage and remarries is no longer entitled to the benefits of the former marriage. In the same way, anyone who leaves Jesus to follow another will no longer receive the honor of inheriting eternal life.

Revelation 21:8 tells us, "But the fearful, and unbelieving, and the abominable, and murderers, and whoremongers, and sorcerers, and idolaters, and all liars, shall have their part in the lake which burneth with fire and brimstone: which is the second death."

All these things represent fruits of unrighteousness.

Revelation 3:5 tells us, "He that overcometh, the same shall be clothed in white raiment; and I will not blot out his name out of the book of life, but I will confess his name before my Father, and before his angels."

Names can be blotted out of the Lamb's Book of Life.

John 14:6 tells us, "Jesus saith unto him, I am the way, the truth, and the life: no man cometh unto the Father, but by me."

Don't tell me that you know God, but you do not believe in Jesus. You will never inherit eternal life. To know Jesus is to know God. To believe in Jesus is to believe in the Father, too.

Acts 4:12 tells us, "Neither is there salvation in any other: for there is none other name under heaven given among men, whereby we must be saved."

If I begin to tell people that I am the Savior of the world, I will end up in hellfire as well as those who follow me because there is only one Savior of the world, and he is Jesus Christ.

Hebrews 1:3-4 tells us, "Who being the brightness of his glory, and the express image of his person, and upholding all things by the word of his power, when he had by himself purged our sins, sat down on the right hand of the Majesty on high: 4 Being made so much better than the angels, as he hath by inheritance obtained a more excellent name than they."

This is the Jesus that I am asking you to give your life to today.

The Jesus who has received more honor than the angels in Heaven.

The Jesus who has more honor than any celebrity or CEO on this earth.

The Jesus who has more honor than any person who is living or has ever lived.

The Jesus who is the brightness of the glory of the Father.

This is the Jesus that I am asking you to follow today.

The Jesus who is the express image of the Father.

The Jesus who is upholding all things by the word of God's power.

The Jesus who died to take away the sins of the world.

The Jesus that created the Heavens and the Earth.

This is the Jesus that I am asking you to believe in today.

The Jesus who said, "Woman thou art loosed," and she was loosed.

The Jesus who can speak words over you and let it come to pass.

The Jesus who is full of grace and truth.

The Jesus who is anointed with the oil of gladness above his fellows because he loves righteousness and hates evil.

This is the Jesus that I am asking you to give your life to today.

The Jesus who brought us to the Father who said, "Be ye holy for I am holy."

The Jesus who was crucified, buried, and risen from the dead.

The Jesus who has gone up into Heaven and is sitting down at the right hand of the Father where angels and authorities and powers are being made subject to him.

This is the Jesus that I am asking you to believe in today.

The Jesus who has been given a name that is above all names.

The Jesus who is full of compassion and mercy.

The Jesus who has the power to forgive all our sins.

John 3:16 tells us, "For God so loved the world, that he gave his only begotten Son, that whosoever believeth in him should not perish, but have everlasting life."

In conclusion, the scriptures resonate with a powerful truth – that Jesus, the Son of God, is the divine Creator of the universe. Through His spoken words, worlds were formed, and by His divine authority, all things were created. This same Jesus, who crafted the intricacies of the cosmos, still holds the power to make things happen today by the word of God. The call echoes forth to believe in Him, to heed His teachings, and to follow His path. The narrative of a woman turning away serves as a cautionary tale, emphasizing the significance of unwavering belief. Yet, there is hope and redemption, for names can be blotted out, but through faith in Jesus, one can overcome and be clothed in righteousness. Let this be an invitation to embrace the Jesus who is the way, the truth, and the life – the one who holds a name above all names and offers forgiveness, compassion, and everlasting life to all who believe. May this message resonate, prompting hearts to repent, confess, and follow the path illuminated by the Son of God, Jesus Christ.

14

The Power of Counsel

Embrace godly counsel, for it not only shapes your journey,
but ensures wisdom in your latter end.

Ungodly counsel not only affects the lives of others, but it also affects you. Psalm 106:43 tells us, "Many times did he deliver them; but they provoked him with their counsel, and were brought low for their iniquity."

God delivered the children of Israel from Pharaoh and the Egyptians, from the Red Sea, and from the bitter waters. When it was time to possess the land that God had given them, Moses was commanded to send chief leaders from each tribe to search the land. However, after searching the land, all of them, except Joshua and Caleb, told the people that they were not able to possess the land.

Their ungodly counsel caused the children of Israel to murmur against Moses and rebel against God. This aroused the anger of God, who led them through the wilderness for 40 years, where those who gave the ungodly counsel died, including those who listened to it.

Ungodly counsel not only affects the lives of others but also impacts you.

Satan told Eve in the Garden of Eden that if she ate the forbidden fruit, she would not surely die, and his ungodly counsel brought judgment upon him, Adam, and Eve.

Ungodly counsel brings judgment, sorrow, and depression, and ultimately, it brings death. If anyone is telling you that you could disobey God and make it to Heaven, God is telling you that you will surely die.

It was the head leaders of the tribes of Israel who misled the people and caused them to miss the promised land. You will not miss the promised land in the name of Jesus.

If anyone is telling you that you are not good enough to do what God has called you to do, here's some godly counsel for you: You might not be good enough, but the God in you is good enough.

If anyone is trying to talk you out of what God has called you to do, here is some godly counsel for you: You can do all things through Christ who strengthens you and makes you good enough.

If anyone is trying to change your destiny, here is some godly counsel for you: Look to the hill from whence cometh your help.

Moses was not good enough to part the Red Sea, but God was good enough. Moses was not good enough to convince Pharaoh to let God's people go, but God was good enough. Moses was not good enough to make the bitter waters sweet, but God was good enough. If God is with you, you are good enough.

James 3:6 tells us, "And the tongue is a fire, a world of iniquity: so is the tongue among our members, that it defileth the whole body, and setteth on fire the course of nature; and it is set on fire of hell.

Don't let your tongue bring you down.

One night, I could not sleep, so I got up to pray. After I prayed, I went back to bed. It was there that the Lord said to me, "Tell people about what will not take them to Heaven." I later shared it with my husband, who immediately released a message about it. Why did he do that? Because he is humble and is ready to do the will of God.

God said to Abraham, "Walk before me and be thou perfect," and Abraham listened to God because he was humble. Are you humble? When God gives you an instruction, do you obey it, or do you rebel against it and make excuses for the wrong that you have done?

Proverbs 12:15 tells us, "The way of a fool is right in his own eyes: but he that hearkeneth unto counsel is wise."

In Luke chapter 18, a very rich ruler came to Jesus for counsel. He wanted to know how to inherit eternal life. Jesus said to him, "You know the commandments, keep them," which is godly counsel for all of us. Then he gave him some personal counsel for himself because he knew that money was an idol in his life and that no idolater would inherit eternal life. So he told him to sell what he had and give it to the poor, and you know what, he could not even give away a penny of what he had. I pray in the name of Jesus Christ that money will not prevent you from entering into the kingdom of Heaven.

Proverbs 19:20 tells us, "Hear counsel, and receive instruction, that thou mayest be wise in thy latter end."

There is going to be a latter end for every one of us, and we had better make ourselves wise by hearing God's counsel and receiving God's instructions. Don't follow the example of the leaders who rejected God's counsel and faced consequences, nor the people who heeded their advice and suffered. Avoid the fate of the very Rich Ruler, who chose his own counsel over Jesus'. Instead, listen to God's guidance and receive His instruction, for it will impart wisdom for the future.

Father, I give you praise, honor, glory, and thank you for this word. Let it be a blessing to the people, but most of all, dear Lord, let it give them wisdom for the future.

15

Blessed are the Peacemakers

Discovering the path of peace begins with embracing
the fear of the Lord.

Matthew 5:9 reminds us, Blessed are the peacemakers, for they shall
be called the children of God." In essence, those who follow the path
of peace are recognized as God's children, while those who choose the
path of conflict are not.

When others label you something other than a child of God, don't
be disheartened. They are simply reflecting what they see. Just as the
fruit of a tree is evident on the outside, so are your actions.

Let me illustrate the actions of those who do not understand the
way of peace. If you've ever engaged in social media, like Twitter, at
a specific time and noticed someone consistently tweeting at the same
time, then adjusted your schedule only to have that person follow your
lead, you've experienced a lack of peace. They mirror your actions in an
attempt to disrupt your peace.

When they tweet behind you, it's akin to pelting stones at a dog, an
act of unwarranted cruelty. This behavior signifies that you are unwel-
come, and it is driven by a spirit of hostility.

I once encountered a situation where, while visiting a friend, I heard the cries of a dog in pain. I discovered that my own dogs were being stoned by someone. Their only offense was being in the wrong place at the wrong time. This act of cruelty, which left me in tears, illustrates Proverbs 12:10: "A righteous man regards the life of his beast, but the tender mercies of the wicked are cruel."

These dogs were innocent, yet they fell victim to cruelty just like me from people who profess to be children of God. The Bible makes it clear that the peacemakers are blessed and recognized as children of God but those who practice such cruelty are not. This is how we are recognized not only by Heaven but also by the world.

Matthew 12:33 underscores the significance of bearing good fruit, emphasizing that a tree is identified by its fruit. Persistent involvement in conflicts, be it on Twitter, Christian media, or elsewhere, constitutes iniquity and may cause you not to inherit eternal life because we are known by our fruits in Heaven.

Matthew 7:21-23 underscores the need to do the will of the Father in heaven, as mere words and actions are insufficient. Those who work iniquity, even while claiming to prophesy or perform miracles, will not enter the kingdom of heaven."

Isaac encountered a similar scenario in Genesis 26. Whenever he dug a well, the Philistines contested it. He moved from one well to another, and they continued to strive against him until he dug a third well, and they finally left him in peace.

I pray in Jesus' name that you will be left in peace to dig your wells. Hold your peace, and let the Lord fight on your behalf, as Isaac did. Resisting the urge to engage in conflict is crucial, as it wastes your time, diverts your focus, and leads to destruction. Remember Jesus' words to Peter: "Put away your sword, for those who take the sword will perish by the sword."

James 3:18 teaches that the fruit of righteousness is sown in peace by peacemakers.

Engaging in conflict with your neighbor prevents the sowing of righteous fruit.

In Isaiah 59:8-9 "The way of peace they know not; and there is no judgment in their goings: they have made them crooked paths: whosoever goeth therein shall not know peace. 9 Therefore is judgment far from us, neither doth justice overtake us: we wait for light, but behold obscurity; for brightness, but we walk in darkness."

The consequences of not knowing peace are vividly described. The passage highlights that those who are unfamiliar with the way of peace are prone to making crooked paths, indicating a deviation from righteous and harmonious living. The absence of judgment and justice in their actions further compounds the issue.

The verses suggest that the lack of adherence to principles of peace leads to a state of moral and spiritual darkness. The people are depicted as waiting for light but finding only obscurity, anticipating brightness but walking in darkness. This metaphorical darkness symbolizes the absence of clarity, righteousness, and divine guidance in their lives.

Overall, the consequences outlined in these verses from Isaiah emphasize the spiritual and moral void that results from straying from the path of peace, leading to a state of confusion, lack of justice, and the absence of divine enlightenment. It also tells us that anyone who chooses to follow this path will never know peace.

When you do not know the way to peace, your prayers may go unanswered, and you may struggle to find deliverance, but when you walk the path of peace, your cries will be heard and answered.

Blessed are the peacemakers, for they shall be called the children of God.

In conclusion, Matthew 5:9 illuminates the blessed status of peacemakers, recognized as children of God. The contrast is stark; those who sow discord are not aligned with the divine identity. Recognition as a child of God goes beyond mere claims and is mirrored in our actions. The illustration of conflict on social media and the poignant example of cruelty to innocent dogs underscore the grave consequences of straying from the path of peace.

The biblical wisdom in Matthew 12:33 emphasizes the vital connection between our actions and eternal destiny, urging us to bear good fruit. The narrative of Isaac's perseverance in Genesis 26 serves as a powerful reminder that holding our peace, trusting the Lord, and avoiding unnecessary conflicts are key to spiritual well-being. As Jesus cautioned Peter, wielding the sword leads to destruction. James 3:18 echoes the importance of sowing righteous fruit through peaceful means, and Isaiah 59:8 warns against the perils of walking crooked paths.

Let the blessing of being called a child of God motivate us to seek and uphold the way of peace, leading to answered prayers and divine guidance. It is a time for repentance and a call to all who seek the way of peace to turn to the Lord and follow it today. May the Lord grant understanding and guide us on the path of peace in Jesus' name.

Bringing Forth the Fruits of the Kingdom

Labor without the righteousness of God is labor in vain. Coveting others' blessings may lead from theft to murder, a perilous path away from righteousness.

Labor without the righteousness of God is labor in vain. Contrary to what you have been taught, God is looking for people who will bring forth the fruits of His kingdom. Matthew 6:33 tells us, "But seek ye first the kingdom of God, and his righteousness; and all these things shall be added unto you."

In the parable of the Wicked Husbandmen, you will see that they were not after the fruits of righteousness but after the inheritance of someone else. They were not interested in the fruits that would cause them to inherit eternal life, but they were after their neighbor's honor, the fruit that would lead to their destruction.

Matthew 21:33-41 tells us, "There was a certain householder, which planted a vineyard, and hedged it round about, and digged a winepress in it, and built a tower, and let it out to husbandmen, and went into a far country: 34 And when the time of the fruit drew near, he sent his servants to the husbandmen, that they might receive the fruits of it. 35 And the husbandmen took his servants, and beat one, and killed another, and stoned another. 36 Again, he sent other servants more than the first: and they did unto them likewise. 37 But last of all, he sent unto them his son, saying, they will reverence my son. 38 But when the husbandmen saw the son, they said among themselves, this is the heir; come, let us kill him, and let us seize on his inheritance. 39 And they caught him, and cast him out of the vineyard, and slew him. 40 When the lord, therefore, of the vineyard cometh, what will he do unto those husbandmen? 41 They say unto him, He will miserably destroy those wicked men, and will let out his vineyard unto other husbandmen, which shall render him the fruits in their seasons."

In this parable, a vineyard was left in the hands of some dishonest, covetous, thieving murderers who refused to release the fruits of the owner at the appointed time. Instead, they made a decision to kill anyone sent to collect the fruits so they could keep the inheritance for themselves. Now you can understand why we have been told not to covet what belongs to our neighbors. Covetous people will become thieves, and thieves will become murderers who will not be marching unto Zion but unto Hell Fire.

Therefore, if you are planning to kill somebody because of their money, my prayer for you is that your evil will not fall upon your own head. If you are planning to kill somebody because of their fruits, my prayer for you is that your evil will not fall upon your own head.

The Wicked Husbandmen in this parable represent the kind of believers in the kingdom whose baskets are full of bad fruits. They work in the vineyard of God 365 days a year, but their baskets are full of fruits such as adultery, fornication, uncleanness, lasciviousness, idolatry, witchcraft, hatred, variance, emulations, wrath, strife, seditions, heresies, envyings, murders, drunkenness, revellings, and such like. Instead of love, joy, peace, longsuffering, gentleness, goodness, faith, meekness, and temperance.

These are the kind of believers who are carnally minded. They are led by their flesh and not by the Spirit of God, and because of this, their focus is on money, lots of money and they do not mind doing anything to get it.

Romans 8:5 tells us, "For they that are after the flesh do mind the things of the flesh; but they that are after the Spirit the things of the Spirit."

They are the kind of believers who labor in the vineyard without the fruits of righteousness and believe that they are on the way to Heaven. I want you to know that God is not interested in labor without the fruits of righteousness.

Labor without the righteousness of God is labor in vain.

Abel was a keeper of sheep, but Cain was a tiller of the ground. 3 And in process of time, it came to pass that Cain brought of the fruit of the ground an offering unto the Lord. 4 And Abel, he also brought of the firstlings of his flock and of the fat thereof. And the Lord had respect unto Abel and to his offering: 5 But unto Cain and to his offering, he had not respect."

They were two laborers who both brought their offerings to the Lord, but one was accepted by God, and the other was rejected because there was no righteousness of God there (Genesis 4:7). Whatever you are doing for the Lord, make sure that the righteousness of God is there, or else it will be rejected by God. I pray that your labor will not be in vain in the name of Jesus.

2 Timothy 2:6 tells us, "The husbandman that laboreth must be first partaker of the fruits. 7 Consider what I say, and the Lord give thee understanding in all things."

In conclusion, this exploration underscores the critical importance of coupling labor with the righteousness of God, as exemplified in the parable of the Wicked Husbandmen. The warning against covetousness, theft, and murder serves as a stark reminder of the perils that befall those who prioritize personal gain over righteousness.

The call to repentance echoes through the narrative, urging believers to align their actions with the fruits of righteousness. The rejection of Cain's offering and the acceptance of Abel's highlight the significance of righteousness in all endeavors. As the biblical admonition goes, labor without the righteousness of God is, indeed, labor in vain. May this reflection inspire a transformative journey towards a labor grounded in righteousness, as believers strive to be first partakers of the fruits in the vineyard of the Lord.

Dear Heavenly Father, I earnestly pray in the powerful name of Jesus that your people will grasp the importance of being first partakers of the fruits of righteousness before serving in your vineyard. This aligns with your divine will for those called to be your servants. If you find yourself serving the Lord without producing the fruits of righteousness, I extend an invitation to repent and turn away from any sinful paths in the name of Jesus. May God's blessings abound upon you.

17

Lusts and the Renewed Mind

Beware the deceitful lusts that lead to sin and death, for true renewal comes through aligning desires with the enduring will of God, not the fleeting allure of worldly cravings.

In a world where distractions and temptations abound, the call to live a life aligned with God's will becomes increasingly crucial. I John 2:17 reminds us that the world and its fleeting desires will pass away, emphasizing the impermanence of worldly pursuits. This article delves into the dangers of yielding to deceitful lusts, drawing insights from biblical narratives like Numbers 11 and cautioning against the pitfalls of looking back to what God has delivered us from. With a focus on renewing the mind through the Word of God and embracing the growth process in the journey of faith, this exploration aims to inspire a commitment to doing the will of God and bearing fruits that endure beyond the transient allure of worldly cravings.

I John 2:17 tells us, "And the world passeth away, and the lust thereof: but he that doeth the will of God abideth forever."

Lusts are described in Ephesians 2:3 as the desires of the flesh and the mind, and we have been told in I John 2:17 that they will pass away with the world--they are temporary things, and we should not invest our

God-given time in them. Instead, we should use our God-given time to do the will of God.

Numbers 11 tells us a story about a group of people who "exceedingly lusted" and were eventually destroyed by God. Their lusting was not one that relates to the sexual, but it was the lusting for food. The Holy Spirit made me understand that they were afraid that they were going to die of hunger, and this caused them to lust for the food of Egypt.

Tell your sisters to be careful of fear. Tell them fear can cause them to lust for the wrong things.

God had provided them with "manna" from heaven for food, but their lack of trust in God and lack of faith in what He was doing in their lives caused them to lust for the food they used to eat in Egypt: the fish, the cucumbers, the melons, the leeks, the onions, and the garlic.

Tell your sisters to be careful of fear. Tell them fear will block their vision of what God is doing. Tell them that whatever God is doing is always greater and better than anything they would find in Egypt.

Tell your sisters to stop lusting after the things of the world. Tell them to desire the things of the kingdom. Tell them, that the food of Egypt may look better, but it isn't better than anything God gives to them. Tell them not to let the lusts of the flesh and the mind destroy them.

Mark 4:18-19 says, "And these are they which are sown among thorns; such as hear the word, 19. And the cares of this world, and the deceitfulness of riches, and the lusts of other things entering in, choke the word, and it becometh unfruitful."

This is the reason God forbids lusting after these things because it makes good seeds become unfruitful by choking the word of God in us.

Choking is not a quick process. It is a slow process which results in the destruction of destiny.

The word of God in the Bible passage represents seeds and seeds represent the knowledge of God. The more knowledge of God we have the more fruits we can produce.

Proverbs 9:10 tells us, "The fear of the Lord is the beginning of wisdom: and the knowledge of the Holy is understanding."

When you have the knowledge of the Holy, you have understanding; when you have understanding you do the things that God tells you to do, and when you do the things that God tells you to do you are bringing forth fruits of growth.

God will take away trees that a not bringing forth the fruits of the kingdom because they do not glory him. John 15:8 tells us that the Father is glorified, when we bear much fruit.

John 15:2 tells us, "Every branch in me that beareth not fruit he taketh away: and every branch that beareth fruit, he purgeth it, that it may bring forth more fruit."

The act of the children of God looking back to Egypt was not merely a mistake; it served as an indication that the children of Israel were not entirely delivered. True deliverance encompasses more than just physical liberation; it involves a transformation of the mind.

In the context of the Bible, the Israelites, after being freed from slavery in Egypt, faced challenges in fully embracing their newfound freedom. Their yearning to return to Egypt was not just a lapse in judgment; it revealed a lingering attachment to the familiarity of their past bondage.

Complete deliverance extends beyond external circumstances and requires a shift in mindset. Liberation becomes meaningful when the mental chains are broken as well. The lesson here is that for total deliverance from any situation, our minds must transform. It involves letting go of old mindsets, perspectives, and attachments that bind us to the past.

A certain group of people in Numbers 11 were destroyed not because they were there physically; but because their minds were still there.

Tell your sisters to stop looking back to the things God moved heaven and earth to save them from. Tell them looking back will lead to their destruction. Tell them that it was their cries that led to their deliverance.

Tell them to remember their cries and stop looking back. Tell them to remember Lot's wife who looked back and was turned into a pillar of salt, but I pray this will not be your portion in the Mighty name of Jesus!

Ephesians 4:22 tells us to "Put off concerning the former conversation the old man, which is corrupt according to the deceitful lusts."

Deceitful lusts corrupt us, without intentionally putting off the old man a believer will find herself following the way of corruption. Our desires need to be in alignment with the will of God. When they are not lined up with the will of God they lead us to sin and death.

James 1:14 tells us, "But every man is tempted, when he is drawn away of his own lust, and enticed. 15 Then when lust hath conceived, it bringeth forth sin: and sin, when it is finished, bringeth forth death."

Deceitful lusts are the fruits of the old man, which believers were commanded to put off; and how do we put him off? We put him off by becoming renewed in the spirit of our minds by the word of God, Ephesians 4:23; and by becoming renewed in the spirit of our minds by the word of God, we put on the new man, Christ, which after God is created in righteousness and true holiness.

If we do not get the spirit of our minds renewed by the word of God, we are not truly born-again. Too many of us only get to the water baptism stage and do not get our minds renewed by the word of God. Too many of us only believe but do not change. There are too many corrupt people naming the name of Jesus and doing corrupt things.

I Peter 23 tells us, "Being born again, not of corruptible seed, but of incorruptible, by the word of God, which liveth and abideth forever."

Another stage of the born-again process is to be born of the word of God.

Ephesians 4:25-32 tells us some of the things we should do to put on the new man, Christ. "Wherefore putting away lying, speak every man truth with his neighbor: for we are members one of another. 26. Be ye angry, and sin not: let not the sun go down upon your wrath: neither give place to the devil. 28. Let him that stole, steal no more: but rather let him labor, working with his hands the thing which is good, that he may have to give to him that needeth. 29. Let no corrupt communication proceed out of your mouth, but that which is good to the use of edifying, that it may minister grace unto the hearers. 30. And grieve not the holy Spirit of God, whereby ye are sealed unto the day of redemption. 31. Let all bitterness, and wrath, and anger, and clamor, and evil speaking, be put away from you, with all malice: 32. And be ye kind one to another, tenderhearted, forgiving one another, even as God for Christ's sake hath forgiven you."

Again, these are things we need to do to put on the new man, Christ Jesus.

I Peter 2:11 tells us, "Dearly beloved, I beseech you as strangers and pilgrims, abstain from fleshly lusts, which war against the soul."

Fleshly lusts war against the soul. What is the soul? The soul is made up of the mind, will, and emotions. It is the part of us that needs to be saved by the word of God. If the soul is not saved, we are not truly born-again. This is the third step of the born-again process. It is the growth process, and it is a true indication that we are walking in a new life.

James 1:24 tells us, "Wherefore lay apart all filthiness and superfluity of naughtiness, and receive with meekness the engrafted word, which is able to save your souls."

Therefore, as we navigate this journey of faith, let us remember that true transformation involves aligning our desires with the timeless will of God. The call to put off deceitful lusts and embrace the renewing power of God's Word remains crucial. May our souls, saved and sanctified, be a testament to the enduring victory found in Christ, who empowers us to walk in the newness of life. Let our lives reflect the genuine fruits of righteousness, bringing glory to the Father and marking us as true disciples of Christ.

18

The Power of a Renewed Mind

Renew your mind, clothe it in the Spirit's wisdom, and journey towards a life adorned with purpose, peace, and victory.

In this insightful exploration, we delve into the profound contrast between the carnal mind, driven by worldly desires, and the spiritual mind, aligned with the teachings of Christ. Drawing from biblical verses, particularly Romans 8, and recounting the lessons from Numbers 11, the narrative underscores the critical importance of renewing one's mind to inherit eternal life. Addressing the influence of our choices on salvation, the article navigates through the pitfalls of carnal-mindedness, discussing the implications of attire choices and emphasizing the significance of spiritual alignment in sowing seeds for everlasting life. Join us on this transformative journey to discern the paths of the flesh and spirit in the pursuit of a life anchored in Christ's teachings.

A certain group of people in Numbers 11 faced destruction because they refused to put on the new man which is renewed in knowledge after the image of God, Col 3:10. They walked after the flesh and obeyed the things of the flesh. This is what the Bible calls to be carnally minded.

Romans 8:7 tells us that the carnal mind is enmity against God: for it is not subject to the law of God neither indeed can be because it is influenced by the flesh and they that are in the flesh cannot please God. Romans 8:6 tells us to be carnally minded is death. Therefore, the carnally minded cannot inherit eternal life.

On the other hand, the spiritual mind or the mind of Christ is the one that will inherit eternal life. The Bible tells us in Philippians 2:5 to let this mind be in you which was in Christ Jesus. It is a humble mind. A mind that is subjected to the law of God and a mind that obeys the things of the Spirit.

Romans 8 tells us that only those who are in Christ have access to this mind. Those who are not in Christ do not have access to this mind because again they are in the flesh, walk after the things of the flesh, and mind the things of the flesh.

But this is not the case and should not be the case for Christians. Romans 8:12-13 tells us, "Therefore, brethren, we are debtors not to the flesh, to live after the flesh. 13. For if ye live after the flesh, ye shall die: but if ye through the Spirit do mortify the deeds of the body, ye shall live. For to be spiritually minded is life and peace," Romans 8:6.

One reason a person may not have peace is because they are not spiritually minded.

Many years ago, I was going somewhere when I saw a young woman who was dressed in a way that made me remember when I used to dress that way. Immediately, the Holy Spirit interjected and reminded me of the Bible verse Romans 8:1 which tells us, "There is therefore now no condemnation to them which are in Christ Jesus who walk not after the flesh, but after the Spirit."

This tells me that there is a way we dress which is influenced by the flesh and there is a way we dress which is influenced by the Spirit. Those who are led by the Spirit find the right way. The way of dressing of the flesh markets the flesh and promotes the flesh, but the way of dressing of the Spirit glorifies the spirit and promotes the Spirit.

I Timothy 2:9-10 tells us, "In like manner also, that women adorn themselves in modest apparel, with shamefacedness and sobriety; not with broided hair, or gold, or pearls, or costly array; 10 But (which becometh women professing godliness) with good works."

Modest dressing represents good work.

Modest means decent. Clothes that do not make you look like a prostitute. Clothes that are not too tight and revealing. Clothes that are long enough for you to bend down and touch your toes without your underwear showing. Clothes that glorify the name of Jesus.

Women get criticized all the time for the clothes they are wearing and are sometimes accused of seducing men; but what about men? They too wear clothes that are too revealing. Jackets tight across the chest and tight on the back and pants tight in the front and the back. These things seduce women, too.

One day I went to a conference with my church and a young minister walked in wearing a suit so tight it revealed his muscular body. As soon as he walked into the hall two sisters in the corner began drooling over him.

The guest minister saw it and proceeded to tell them what kind of spirit was manifesting in them. I saw it too and I said to myself, "Why is his jacket so tight?" And that was not the last time I saw a man dressed inappropriately. The way women and men dress should glorify Jesus and love will not dress in a way to make its neighbor fall.

Matthew 7:13-14 tells us to "Enter ye in at the strait gate: for wide is the gate, and broad is the way, that leadeth to destruction, and many there be which go in thereat:14 Because strait is the gate, and narrow is the way, which leadeth unto life, and few there be that find it."

Jesus told the religious leaders of his time that if they did not believe that he was the son of God, they would die in their sins. I want to let you know that if you do not believe that Jesus is the son of God and the Savior of the world you too will die in your sins John 8:24. It is time to repent and give your life to him.

The children of Israel were God's children, but some were led by the lusts of their flesh and their carnal minds, and some were led by the Spirit of God and their spiritual minds. It is the same with many people in the body of Christ today. Some are led by the flesh, and some are led by the Spirit. Some sow to the flesh and will reap corruption; and some sow to the Spirit and will reap life everlasting, Galatians 6:8.

In conclusion, as we navigate the intricate paths of life, let us earnestly strive to renew our minds daily, casting away the garments of the flesh and embracing thc wardrobe of the Spirit. May our choices in attire reflect not only modesty but also a deep reverence for the sanctity of our bodies, and may we walk the narrow way that leads to life everlasting, guided by the Spirit, our minds renewed, and our lives transformed in the image of Christ.

19

The Heavens Rule

It is better to embrace humility and walk with God willingly,
than to endure the consequences of pride.

In a world often marked by pride and power struggles, ancient wisdom from 2 Chronicles 7:14 provides a timeless guide for those seeking healing and divine intervention. This verse emphasizes the transformative power of humility, prayer, and turning away from wickedness to attract the attention and favor of the heavens. Drawing inspiration from the biblical narrative of King Nebuchadnezzar, whose pride led to a humbling experience, and contrasting it with the humility exemplified by Jesus, we explore the profound impact of recognizing and honoring the Most High God in our lives. Join us on a journey of reflection and rediscovery as we delve into the importance of humility in the context of faith, prayer, and divine guidance.

2 Chronicles 7:14 says, "If my people, who are called by my name, shall humble themselves, and pray, and seek my face, and turn from their wicked ways; then will I hear from heaven, and will forgive their sin, and will heal their land."

To be humble means to rid yourself of pride and obey God. It is the crucial first step in gaining Heaven's attention during prayer. Prayer itself doesn't bring humility, but eliminating pride and obeying God makes prayer effective. When this happens, prayer reaches God, and He heals the land.

Prideful people cannot get God to heal a headache, let alone heal a nation. Their prayers are like balls thrown against a wall; they bounce back.

However, Elijah's prayer was different; he prayed for no rain for three and a half years, and it did not rain. Then he prayed again for rain, and it fell. A prideful and wicked person cannot achieve this.

Proverbs 8:13 tells us, "The fear of the Lord is to hate evil: pride, arrogance, the evil way, and the forward mouth, do I hate."

Where there is pride, there is wickedness, but humble people depart from evil.

King Nebuchadnezzar was a great king honored by God, but when his heart was lifted in pride, his glory was taken away. He lived like an animal until he learned that the Most High God rules in the kingdom of men.

Therefore, if any king is trying to stop God's glory in your life or change God's plan, this message is to remind them that, the Heavens rule. If any king is fighting against God's will for you, this message is to declare that the Heavens rule.

Nebuchadnezzar, heartless and warned by Daniel, showed no mercy to the poor by robbing them. On the contrary, Jesus, humble and caring for the poor preached kindness to the poor and told people to give to them.

Humble people honor God. Humble people recognize God. Humble people respect God.

Nebuchadnezzar used his tongue to disrespect God when he said in Daniel 3:15, "Now if ye be ready that at what time ye hear the sound of the cornet, flute, harp, sackbut, psaltery, and dulcimer, and all kinds of music, ye fall down and worship the image which I have made; well (meaning it shall be well with you): but if ye worship not, ye shall be cast the same hour into the midst of a burning fiery furnace; and who is that God that shall deliver you out of my hands?"

Maybe somebody somewhere is making this kind of bold declaration over you, so I came to let you know that the Most High God of Heaven can deliver you out of their hands just like he delivered his children from the hands of King Nebuchadnezzar in the book of Daniel.

The Most High God of Heaven was revealed to King Nebuchadnezzar when he could not remember a dream that he had, which none of his magicians were able to reveal. So, God used his servant Daniel not only to tell him what the dream was but also to interpret the dream. Instead of giving honor to the God of heaven, he came up with an idea to build a golden image to worship.

My prayer for you is that when God is revealing himself to you, you will not ignore Him.

Nebuchadnezzar had no problem worshipping Daniel. He had no problem worshipping other gods, but when it came to worshipping the Most High God of Heaven, he had a problem with it. This is the God who gave him all that he had.

Luke 4:8 tells us, "And Jesus answered and said unto him, Get thee behind me, Satan: for it is written, Thou shalt worship the Lord thy God, and him only shalt thou serve."

Maybe you are like King Nebuchadnezzar, you worship yourself, you worship people, and you worship idols, but you do not worship the Most High God of Heaven in whose hands is your breath. It is time to humble yourself, repent, and give Him the honor that He is worthy of.

Psalm 96:7 tells us, "Give unto the Lord, O ye kindreds of the people, give unto the Lord glory and strength. 8 Give unto the Lord the glory due unto his name: bring an offering, and come into his courts. 9 O worship the Lord in the beauty of holiness: fear before him, all the earth."

Don't be like King Nebuchadnezzar; decide to worship the God of Heaven today.

Next, Nebuchadnezzar used his tongue once again to disrespect God in Daniel 4:30 when he said, "Is not this great Babylon, that I have built for the house of the kingdom by the might of my power, and for the honour of my majesty?"

He was saying that he was the one who built the kingdom by his strength, and he was the one who gave himself his honor. He never recognized the mighty hands of the Most High God in his success.

I pray that you will not be this kind of person, but you will recognize the hand of God in your life.

People who are not humble always think that all they have is from their strength, abilities, or special qualities and they never remember to give praise and honor to the Most High God of Heaven who blessed them. But after King Nebuchadnezzar was made to live like an animal outside for several years, he remembered to praise, honor, and recognize the Most High God of Heaven for all that he did for him.

And this is what he said after he was restored in Daniel 4:37, "Now I Nebuchadnezzar praise and extol and honour the King of heaven, all whose works are truth, and his ways judgment: and those that walk in pride he is able to abase."

Nebuchadnezzar realized that he did not rule, but it was the Heavens that ruled: and it is better to humble yourself before God than to be full of pride and receive judgment.

Micah 6:8 tells us, "He hath shewed thee, O man, what is good; and what doth the Lord require of thee, but to do justly, and to love mercy, and to walk humbly with thy God?"

God is asking someone to walk humbly with Him today.

In conclusion, the ageless lessons drawn from biblical narratives and timeless principles underscore the profound significance of humility in our spiritual journey. Whether facing the challenges of pride, as exemplified by King Nebuchadnezzar, or embracing the compassionate humility embodied by Jesus, the call remains clear—to walk humbly with our Creator. The wisdom of 2 Chronicles 7:14 continues to echo through the ages, reminding us that healing and divine intervention follow the path of humility, prayer, and turning from wicked ways. As we navigate the complexities of life, may we heed this call to honor, recognize, and respect the Most High God, finding solace and restoration in the understanding that true rulership lies in the hands of the heavens.

20

Faith Like My Chocolate Cake

Much like a freshly baked chocolate cake, a perfected faith emerges from the oven as a flawless masterpiece, complete and lacking nothing.

When I bake a chocolate cake, my eager children can't resist grabbing large chunks of it while it's still warm, leaving the cake with missing pieces. This scene reminds me of 1 Thessalonians 3:10, where the Apostle Paul conveyed his sentiments:

"Night and day praying exceedingly that we might see your face, and might perfect that which is lacking in your faith."

The Apostle Paul fervently desired to meet the Thessalonian believers. He was concerned that his work with them might have been in vain, and he worried that the tempter may have tempted them. He prayed unceasingly for an opportunity to see how they were living the Christian life, with the goal of perfecting their faith.

Though they had received praise for their love for one another, the Apostle Paul urged them to increase and abound even more in their love for fellow believers, emphasizing the importance of loving believers of all nationalities.

In his efforts to perfect their faith, he comforted them regarding the afflictions they were appointed to face. In times of pain and suffering, it's comforting to have someone like the Apostle Paul offering words of encouragement, rather than insensitive individuals like Job's friends who exacerbated his suffering with their words.

Mark 8:35 states: "For whosoever will save his life shall lose it; but whosoever shall lose his life for my sake and the gospel's, the same shall save it." This verse signifies that the cross, representing the burdens, afflictions, and suffering, is a part of every believer's journey.

Finally, the Apostle Paul prayed for the Thessalonians, as revealed in 1 Thessalonians 3:11-13: "Now God himself and our Father, and our Lord Jesus Christ, direct our way unto you. And the Lord make you to increase and abound in love one toward another, and toward all men, even as we do toward you: To the end he may stablish your hearts unblameable in holiness before God, even our Father, at the coming of our Lord Jesus Christ with all his saints."

This prayer highlights the aim of perfecting believers' faith, which is to prepare their hearts as unblameable in holiness for the return of Christ Jesus.

Additional guidance is found in 1 Peter 2:1-3:
"Wherefore laying aside all malice, and all guile, and hypocrisies, and envies, and all evil speakings, as newborn babes, desire the sincere milk of the word, that ye may grow thereby: If so be ye have tasted that the Lord is gracious."

And in 2 Peter 3:18:
"But grow in grace, and in the knowledge of our Lord and Saviour Jesus Christ. To him be glory both now and forever. Amen."

God's vision for His people is their growth in all aspects in Christ Jesus. The Apostle Paul employed teaching, warnings, and prayer to fulfill this vision.

A perfected faith, much like my freshly baked chocolate cake, emerges from the oven as a flawless masterpiece, complete and lacking nothing.

May this message bless you, and may it forever reside in your heart. In Jesus' mighty name, we say, Amen.

21

The Stone Was Rolled Away

The Lord said, the stone blocking your path is rolled away and you are free indeed!

Mark 16:1-4 tells us:

"And when the sabbath was past, Mary Magdalene, and Mary the mother of James, and Salome, had bought sweet spices, that they might come and anoint him. 2 And very early in the morning the first day of the week, they came unto the sepulchre at the rising of the sun. 3 And they said among themselves, Who shall roll us away the stone from the door of the sepulchre? 4 And when they looked, they saw that the stone was rolled away: for it was very great."

The Lord sent me to tell you that the stone was rolled away. The stone that Satan placed in your way to imprison you and to keep you caged was rolled away. The Lord said he sent an angel to take it away and to loose you from the prison of the enemy. The battle is over. You have been set free. And whom the Son sets free is free indeed.

I know that you know this story very well. After they crucified Jesus, a great stone was placed at His tomb to imprison him just in case he rose again, and soldiers were also instructed to guard it day and night but despite this, God sent an angel, and the stone was rolled away.

It was rumored that he would rise again on the third day, prompting Satan to devise a plan. How many among you are aware that Satan schemes against your rights and freedom?

When the angel from God appeared, the soldiers were rendered mere puppets, and the substantial stone was effortlessly rolled away. After all, there is no stone too great that God cannot move, no problem too big that God cannot solve, and no sickness too great that God cannot heal because nothing is too difficult for Him.

Luke 13:11-12 tells us,
"And, behold, there was a woman which had a spirit of infirmity eighteen years, and was bowed together, and could in no wise lift up herself. 12 And when Jesus saw her, he called her to him, and said unto her, "Woman, thou art loosed from thine infirmity.""

I don't know who I am talking to, but the Lord is saying, "Woman thou art loosed!" No more chains, no more bondage, no more imprisonment, no more bewitchment, no more infirmity, says the Lord. You are loosed!

When you look at the purpose of Satanic prisons, you will discover that prisons come to take away your praise. Prisons come to bring reproach. Prisons come to bring you sorrow. Prisons come to bring you burdens. Prisons come to stop the manifestation of the glory of God in your life. Prisons come to deny you your rights and limit you.

The Woman with the Spirit of infirmity was bound for eighteen years by Satan, but the end to her imprisonment came, and the end to your imprisonment has come too. She was bent over and was trying to lift up herself for eighteen years day after day after day; night after night after night, but she couldn't until Jesus came and restored her with His words.

The Lord has restored you with His words. You have been set free. The infirmity is gone, and the stone has been rolled away, says the Spirit of the Lord.

John 3:16
"For God so loved the world, that he gave his only begotten Son, that whosoever believeth in him should not perish, but have everlasting life. Give your life to Jesus, He wants to set you free from prisons, too.

22

Beware of Flattery

Beware the sweet poison of flattery; it seeks to steal your worth. Trust in God's protection, for a sincere heart holds more value than deceptive praise.

The Lord has tasked me to forewarn you about the dangers of flattery. An illustrative example of flattery is depicted in Aesop's Fable titled "The Fox and the Crow.

In this fable, a crow perched on a branch with a piece of cheese in her mouth encountered a fox. The fox, employing flattery, praised her beauty and wondered if her voice matched her appearance.

Now, if you're well-versed in bird species, you'd know that a crow is distinct from a Common Loon, an Orange-winged Amazon, a Mockingbird, a Veery, a Malabar Whistling Thrush, a Whistling Cockatiel, a Canary, an Asian Koel, or a Nightingale. A crow isn't typically celebrated for its singing prowess.

Despite this, upon hearing the fox's words, the crow opened her mouth to sing, uttering a simple "CAW," causing the cheese to fall into the waiting mouth of the sly fox.

Just as in the fable, there are individuals out there aiming to steal the metaphorical cheese from your mouth. God is cautioning you against succumbing to their flattery, as the crow did in the fable.

I understand that you may yearn for affirmation, even from unlikely sources like a deceptive dirty fox. God is emphatically pre-warning you not to be deceived by lies and flattery.

A fox, in this context, symbolizes someone who harbors ill thoughts about you, viewing you as a naive and easy target. God's pre-warning is clear: do not be swayed by their flattery.

Always remember that contrary to the opinions of foxes, God values a singing crow with a pure heart over a singing Nightingale with an impure heart.

Proverbs 26:28 enlightens us: "A lying tongue hates those it hurts, and a flattering mouth works ruin."

Flattery is a destructive force that arises from someone's hatred and seeks to steal what rightfully belongs to you. In the eyes of the Lord, flattery is not a virtuous trait; it is considered iniquity.

Proverbs 29:5 warns, "A man who flatters his neighbor spreads a net for his feet."

You should be aware that someone who flatters you is likely seeking to harm you, as a flattering tongue is often laden with lies and deceit. God is advising you to exercise caution around those with flattering tongues.

Psalm 36:2 underscores the danger of self-flattery: "For he flatters himself in his own eyes, until his iniquity be found to be hateful."

When the fox took the cheese from the crow, he might have felt clever, but God's judgment considered his behavior hateful and impending. The Lord is not blind to such actions.

Job 17:5 reminds us: "He who speaks flattery to his friends will ultimately cause the eyes of his children to fail." Psalm 12:3 adds, "The Lord shall cut off all flattering lips and the tongue that speaks proud things."

God has decreed a woe upon the offspring of flatterers, so those who engage in flattery are not exempt from divine judgment.

Psalm 12:5 assures that God will rise against the flatterers of your life, bringing you to a place of safety and protection.

The poor crow in the fable may have regretted her foolishness, but God heard her cries and defended her. Likewise, God will rise to your defense in the face of flattery, ensuring your safety and well-being. In the mighty name of Jesus Christ, His protection will be yours.

23

Buy the Truth and Receive Freedom through Repentance

Embrace the truth, for in it lies the path to freedom and honor. Let repentance be your compass, leading you back to the Father's house where true deliverance awaits.

In Acts chapter 7, Stephen, a child of God full of the Holy Ghost, wisdom, and faith, was stoned to death because of the truth. We are living in times when people do not want to hear the truth. Just tell them the truth, and you may face persecution.

But what did Jesus say about the truth? He said, "If ye continue in my word, then are ye my disciples indeed; And ye shall know the truth, and the truth shall make you free," John 8:31-32.

Jesus emphasized that the truth sets us free, and continuity in walking according to God's word leads to freedom. Here is an example of a church in the Bible that deviated from the truth and was commanded to repent.

Revelation 3:14-22 says, "And unto the angel of the church of the Laodiceans write: These things saith the Amen, the faithful and true witness, the beginning of the creation of God; I know thy works, that thou art neither cold nor hot: I would thou wert cold or hot. So then because thou art lukewarm, and neither cold nor hot, I will spue thee out of my mouth. Because thou sayest, I am rich, and increased with goods, and have need of nothing; and knowest not that thou art wretched, and miserable, and poor, and blind, and naked: I counsel thee to buy of me gold tried in the fire, that thou mayest be rich; and white raiment, that thou mayest be clothed, and that the shame of thy nakedness do not appear; and anoint thine eyes with eye salve, that thou mayest see. As many as I love, I rebuke and chasten: be zealous, therefore, and repent. Behold, I stand at the door, and knock: if any man hear my voice and open the door, I will come in to him, and will sup with him, and he with me. To him that overcometh will I grant to sit with me in my throne, even as I also overcame and am set down with my Father in his throne. He that hath an ear, let him hear what the Spirit saith unto the churches."

This church boasted about its wealth, but God declared them wretched, poor, miserable, blind, and naked. They had departed from the truth, abandoning the path of righteousness and holiness. God labeled them lukewarm and counseled them to buy gold tried in the fire for true riches and white raiment to cover the shame of their nakedness.

Obedience to God's counsel would lead to their deliverance and freedom, but disobedience would result in their destruction and dishonor, denying them the honor of sitting with Jesus on His throne.

Your deliverance and honor will come through repentance.

In John 8:34-35 "Jesus said, Verily, verily, I say unto you, Whosoever committeth sin is the servant of sin. And the servant abideth not in the house forever: but the Son abideth ever."

An example of this is found in the parable of the prodigal son in Luke 15, where a man had two sons. One remained in his house forever, but the other left his father's house and became a servant of sin. When he came to his senses, he returned to his father's house, where his father celebrated his return.

It is time to repent and come back to your Father's house!

Luke 15:7 tells us, "I say unto you, that likewise joy shall be in heaven over one sinner that repenteth, more than over ninety and nine just persons, which need no repentance."

John 8:36 tells us, "If the Son, therefore, shall make you free, ye shall be free indeed."

Today, I pray that, like the prodigal son, you will truly be made free. I pray that you will come to your senses and return to your Father's house in the name of Jesus before it is too late.

In conclusion, the narratives from Acts chapter 7, John 8, Revelation 3, and Luke 15 collectively emphasize the profound significance of adhering to the truth and the consequences of straying from God's path. Stephen's martyrdom illustrates the challenges of speaking the truth in a world resistant to it. Jesus' words underscore the liberating power of the truth and the freedom attained through obedience to His teachings. The Laodicean church serves as a cautionary tale, highlighting the perils of spiritual lukewarmness and departure from God's truth. The call to repentance echoes through these passages, emphasizing the transformative power of returning to the Father's house, exemplified in the parable of the prodigal son. As we navigate a world that often rejects the truth, these biblical teachings encourage us to stand firm, embrace repentance, and find true freedom in obedience to God's Word.

24

You Don't Have to Die: Embrace the Giver of Eternal Life and Live

Recognize the identity of Jesus, embrace His promises, and let your belief pave the way for miracles. In Him, eternal life is not a distant hope but a gift within your reach.

Many people may not inherit eternal life because they do not believe in who Jesus is. Jesus, during His time on Earth, devoted Himself to convincing people that He was the Messiah foretold by the prophets and that He was sent by the Father.

Isaiah 9:6 states:
"For unto us a child is born, unto us a son is given: and the government shall be upon his shoulder: and his name shall be called Wonderful, Counsellor, The mighty God, The everlasting Father, The Prince of Peace."

Psalm 110:1 says:
"The Lord said unto my Lord, 'Sit thou at my right hand, until I make thine enemies thy footstool."

When Lazarus died, it was the perfect time to reveal the manifestation of the glory of God so that people might believe. Jesus received news that His friend Lazarus was sick, but by the time He arrived, Lazarus was dead and had been buried for four days.

Upon reaching the scene, Jesus met Martha, who expressed that if He had been there, her brother would not have died. It was then that Jesus said to her, "I am the resurrection and the life: he that believeth in me, though he were dead, yet shall he live: 26 And whosoever liveth and believeth in me shall never die. Believest thou this?" And Martha replied, "Yea, Lord: I believe that thou art the Christ, the Son of God which should come into the world," John 11:25-27.

Jesus aimed to dispel the doubt He observed in Martha. She did not believe her brother could be resurrected after being dead for four days until he was brought back to life.

What about you? Have you been doubting what your Lord can do? Have you questioned His words? Do you believe He will do what He said He will do? It is time for you to believe. Do not let your unbelief obstruct your miracle today.

In John 11:39-45, "Jesus said, "Take ye away the stone." Martha, the sister of the dead, said, "Lord, by this time he stinketh: for he hath been dead four days." Jesus responded, "Said I not unto thee, that, if thou wouldest believe, thou shouldest see the glory of God?" They took away the stone, and Jesus, lifting up His eyes, said, "Father, I thank thee that thou hast heard me. And I knew that thou hearest me always: but because of the people which stand by I said it, that they may believe that thou hast sent me." He cried with a loud voice, "Lazarus, come forth." And he that was dead came forth, bound hand and foot with graveclothes: and his face was bound about with a napkin.

Jesus said unto them, "Loose him, and let him go." Then many of the Jews who came to Mary and had seen the things which Jesus did, believed in him."

Today, Jesus is still doing the same thing from Heaven. He is seeking those who will believe in Him so that He can set them free.

The message Jesus is conveying to you right now is: You don't have to die. You can live forever with Him in eternity.

Romans 6:23 tells us, "For the wages of sin is death; but the gift of God is eternal life through Jesus Christ our Lord."

John 3:16 declares, "For God so loved the world, that he gave his only begotten Son, that whosoever believeth in him should not perish, but have everlasting life."

It is time to repent, believe in the name of Jesus, and follow him.

In conclusion, the story of Lazarus serves as a powerful testament to the unwavering faith and miraculous capabilities of Jesus Christ. His declaration, "I am the resurrection and the life," echoes through time, inviting us to confront our doubts and embrace the transformative power of belief. Just as Jesus called Lazarus from the tomb, He continues to call us today, urging us to shed the graveclothes of unbelief and step into the freedom of eternal life. The message is clear: You don't have to succumb to the grip of death; instead, through faith in Jesus Christ, you can experience the gift of everlasting life. May this truth resonate in our hearts, inspiring a renewed commitment to repentance, belief, and obedience to our Savior, who extends His invitation to life beyond the grave.

25

Lewd Fellows of a Baser Sort

Embrace and apply the word of God, for therein lies
spiritual nobility.

In Acts 17, the Apostle Paul embarked on a journey to a Jewish
synagogue in Thessalonica, where he engaged in a series of discussions
with the people. For three consecutive Sabbath days, he reasoned from
the scriptures, emphasizing that Jesus is the Christ and that His purpose
involved suffering and resurrection from the dead.

As Paul concluded his visit, a significant number of individuals em-
braced the message of Jesus. However, there were also Jewish dissenters
who, fueled by envy due to the attention bestowed upon Paul, gathered
a group described as "lewd fellows of a baser sort." This unruly assembly
incited chaos within the city, launching an attack on the house where
the Apostle Paul was staying. Their actions stirred animosity against
Paul, compelling him to flee to the city of Berea.

In Berea, Paul found himself in another Jewish synagogue, this
time encountering a distinct group of people. He commended them as
"more noble" than those in Thessalonica, explaining that they received
the word with open hearts and actively sought to validate the teachings
by daily scrutiny of the scriptures.

Acts 17:11 notes this distinction:
"These were more noble than those in Thessalonica, in that they received the word with all readiness of mind, and searched the scriptures daily, whether those things were so."

Within the realm of churches and Christian organizations, two distinct groups of individuals can be identified: those characterized by a 'baser sort' with poor moral character, and those who exhibit a 'more noble' disposition with excellent moral character. The former group includes those who do not receive the word of God with all readiness of mind and do not search the scriptures daily to verify the truth of what they are being taught, while the latter group consists of individuals who actively engage in these practices.

Ezekiel 16:52 highlights the disparities between individuals and their moral conduct. Some, like Jerusalem, may commit sins deemed more abominable than those of others. Similarly, among the children of God, some demonstrate greater honor, virtue, and righteousness, with Christ serving as the ultimate exemplar of righteousness. This distinction stems from their willingness to not only hear the word of God but to put it into action.

James 1:22 emphasizes the significance of translating faith into action: "But be ye doers of the word, and not hearers only, deceiving your own selves."

In summary, Acts 17 reveals the contrasting hearts within the faith: those who readily receive the word and diligently explore its truth and those who do not. The path to spiritual nobility and righteousness lies in embracing the word of God and putting it into practice, as exemplified by Christ and the noble believers in Berea.

26

Who Are Liars?

In God's truth we speak, in His light, we walk, and with genuine love, our journey unfolds toward eternal life.

Liars Speak Their Own Words.

Liars speak their own words, as John 8:44 tells us, "Ye are of your father the devil, and the lusts of your father ye will do. He was a murderer from the beginning, and abode not in the truth because there is no truth in him. When he speaketh a lie, he speaketh of his own: for he is a liar, and the father of it."

Years ago, a friend came to my house and began explaining why I was going through a challenging time. Before she could finish, the Holy Spirit told me it was a lie. Why? Because she spoke from her own mind, not God's. Speaking assumptions or guesses about others without God's guidance makes us liars. We should never bring messages that God did not give us.

Jesus spoke the Father's words, not His own, as John 14:10 states, "Believest thou not that I am in the Father, and the Father in me? The words that I speak unto you I speak not of myself: but the Father that dwelleth in me, he doeth the works." Speaking the Father's words is speaking the truth.

Liars say that they have Fellowship with God but Walk in Darkness.

I John 1:6-7 states, "If we say that we have fellowship with him and walk in darkness, we lie, and do not the truth: But if we walk in the light, as he is in the light, we have fellowship one with another, and the blood of Jesus Christ his Son cleanseth us from all sin."

Claiming fellowship with God while persistently walking in darkness is falsehood. Not keeping God's commandments, mentioned in 1 John 2:4, makes one a liar, with Revelation 21:8 warning of the consequences for all liars.

Here are some Examples of Walking in Darkness:

- Using spiritual gifts to steal from others.
- Resorting to witchcraft to invade the lives of others and obstruct destinies.
- Falsely claiming divine revelation when influenced by demonic forces.
- Utilizing Satanic power for wrongdoing.
- Engaging in theft and unrighteous actions.
- Bullying.

Liars say that they Love God, but they Hate the Brethren.

1 John 4:20-21 tells us, "If a man say, I love God, and hateth his brother, he is a liar: for he that loveth not his brother whom he hath seen, how can he love God whom he hath not seen? And this commandment have we from him, That he who loveth God love his brother also."

Perfect love includes loving God and the brethren as well. Ungodly acts of hatred against the brethren do not demonstrate love for God, and whenever this happens, the Bible calls us liars because we cannot say that we love God but do not love the brethren. Taking away all that someone has is not love.

As we draw the curtains on this exploration of truth and deception, the article "Who Are Liars?" beckons us to examine the roots and consequences of falsehood in our lives. From the revealing nature of words spoken without divine guidance to the paradox of claiming fellowship with God while walking in darkness, and the profound impact of love intertwined with genuine fellowship, the scriptures serve as a timeless guide. Let the lessons of discernment and authenticity resonate within, urging us towards a path illuminated by God's truth, light, and love. May the pursuit of eternal life be marked by sincerity, forsaking the shadows of falsehood, and embracing the authentic journey of faith. In the name of Jesus, may our lives be a testament to the genuine love and fellowship that He exemplified.

Confidence in God

Always place your unwavering confidence in the Living God. He remains the unchanging Savior, Deliverer, and Healer.

Embarking on a profound exploration of the Epistle to the Hebrews, we delve into the intricacies of Hebrews 3, a chapter that unfolds critical insights into the Christian journey. The scripture beckons us to consider Jesus, the Apostle, and High Priest of our profession, drawing parallels between His faithfulness and that of Moses. The conditional nature of our relationship with Christ is woven into the narrative, challenging us to hold fast to our confidence and rejoice in hope unto the end. As we navigate the passages, we encounter warnings against unbelief and exhortations to one another, emphasizing the daily counsel needed to combat the deceitfulness of sin. Join us in this illuminating exploration as we glean wisdom from Hebrews 3, seeking to anchor our faith securely in Christ amidst life's challenges.

Hebrews 3:1-6 tells us, "Wherefore, holy brethren, partakers of the heavenly calling, consider the Apostle and High Priest of our profession, Christ Jesus; 2 Who was faithful to him that appointed him, as also Moses was faithful in all his house. 3 For this man was counted worthy of more glory than Moses, inasmuch as he who hath builded the house hath more honour than the house. 4 For every house is builded by some man; but he that built all things is God. 5 And Moses verily was faithful in all his house, as a servant, for a testimony of those things which were to be spoken after; 6 But Christ as a son over his own house; whose house are we, if we hold fast the confidence and the rejoicing of the hope firm unto the end."

When I was in school, I learned that the word "if" is conditional. For example, if you come to class on time, you will get a treat which means that if you do not come to class on time, you will not get a treat.

In the same way, Hebrews 3:6 tells us that we can only be Christ's house if we hold fast the confidence and the rejoicing of the hope firm unto the end. If we do not hold fast the confidence and the rejoicing of the hope firm unto the end, we will no longer be Christ's house. In other words, Christ will no longer dwell in us. It is conditional.

Hebrews 3:7-11 tells us, "Wherefore (as the Holy Ghost saith, Today if ye will hear his voice, 8 Harden not your hearts, as in the provocation, in the day of temptation in the wilderness: 9 When your fathers tempted me, proved me, and saw my works forty years. 10 Wherefore I was grieved with that generation, and said, they do always err in their heart; and they have not known my ways. 11 So I sware in my wrath, they shall not enter into my rest.)"

Pray this prayer. I will not be a part of the generation who always err in their hearts and do not know the ways of the Lord. I reject it. I will enter into my rest in the mighty name of Jesus.

Hebrews 3:12 tells us, "Take heed, brethren, lest there be in any of you an evil heart of unbelief, in departing from the living God."

Unbelief in God is evil. Unbelief in God will lead you to hellfire. Unbelief in God will cause you to depart from the faith and God.

Hebrews 3:13 says, "But exhort one another daily, while it is called today; lest any of you be hardened through the deceitfulness of sin."

We are not doing the will of God if we are not exhorting the brethren daily. Counsel is used to prevent the brethren from being hardened by the deceitfulness of sin—something that makes them feel good but that is leading them to destruction.

Hebrews 3:14 tells us, "For we are made partakers of Christ, if we hold the beginning of our confidence stedfast unto the end."

This is another conditional statement. We cannot be made partakers of Christ if we do not hold the beginning of our confidence steadfast until the end. Or continue believing to the end.

Let's say that I started doubting that Jesus is the Saviour of the world. Do you think I will still make it into Heaven? Let's say I start doubting that there is a living God. Do you think that I will still make it into Heaven? This is the sin of unbelief. Whenever this is happening, just know that you are being set up for destruction.

When I got baptized with water, I felt a great presence with me which I had never felt before my baptism. How can I, who had this experience, allow the devil to put doubt into my heart about God? That experience made me know that God really exists.

2 Corinthians 1:8-10 tells us, "For we would not, brethren, have you ignorant of our trouble which came to us in Asia, that we were pressed out of measure, above strength, insomuch that we despaired even of life: 9 But we had the sentence of death in ourselves, that we should not

trust in ourselves, but in God which raiseth the dead: 10 Who delivered us from so great a death, and doth deliver: in whom we trust that he will yet deliver us."

The apostles, despite their trouble, did not put trust in themselves but held on to their confidence in God to deliver them because he had delivered them before, so they were now able to tell others that he does deliver.

God delivers. He delivered me and my family members many times, and he will deliver you, too.

In concluding this reflection on the profound teachings of Hebrews 3, let us grasp the essence of holding steadfast to our confidence in Christ. The conditional nature of our relationship with Him is highlighted—our dwelling in His house depends on our unwavering commitment. The scriptural warning against an evil heart of unbelief underscores the gravity of trusting in God. As we navigate the challenges of life, let us heed the call to encourage one another daily, preventing the deceitfulness of sin from hardening our hearts. The article beckons us to hold firm from the beginning to the end, acknowledging the conditional promises woven into our spiritual journey. May this insight guide us toward a resilient faith, ensuring that we remain partakers of Christ, ever trusting in His delivering power.

28

Expressing Gratitude for the Father's Blessings

The Father has bestowed remarkable blessings upon us. Let us offer our heartfelt gratitude for all that He has done.

In Psalm 92:1 and Colossians 2:13-15, gratitude and victory intertwine, emphasizing the transformative power of Jesus Christ. Without Him, sins linger unforgiven, and spiritual adversaries remain undefeated. Luke 10:17-20 reveals the authority bestowed upon believers, echoed in personal experiences of overcoming spiritual challenges. Amidst choruses of gratitude, the passages guide us to rejoice not in earthly achievements but in our eternal names written in Heaven. Corinthians and Romans promise a day of universal rejoicing in the ultimate triumph through Christ's sacrifice. Today, as we acknowledge this reality, we stand as more than conquerors through Christ's boundless love. Glory Hallelujah!

Psalm 92:1 says, "It is a good thing to give thanks unto the Lord and to sing praises unto thy name, O Most High. Today is a good day for all believers to give thanks to God for all that He has done for us through His Son Jesus Christ."

Colossians 2:13-15 states, "And you, being dead in your sins and the uncircumcision of your flesh, hath he quickened together with him, having forgiven you all trespasses; 14 Blotting out the handwriting of ordinances that was against us, which was contrary to us, and took it out of the way, nailing it to his cross; 15 And having spoiled principalities and powers, he made a show of them openly, triumphing over them in it."

Without Jesus, none of our sins would be forgiven. Without Jesus, none of the written woes, curses, spells, and words of bewitchment against us would be blotted out. Without Jesus, we would have no victory over demons, devils, principalities, and powers, but because of Him, we have victory over them.

One day the Lord opened my eyes to see a serpent crawling on my head in the spirit, so I just placed my hand around it and squeezed the life out of it without any stress. This is an example of the power that we have been given, but Jesus told us not to rejoice in the fact that the spirits are subject to us but rejoice that our names are written in Heaven.

Rejoicing in our gifts is meaningless because all that we have is given to us. Rejoicing because of our education is meaningless because it cannot take us to heaven. Rejoicing in our wealth is meaningless because one day we will leave it all behind, or it will all fly away, and rejoicing in our beauty is meaningless because beauty is vain.

Luke 10:17-20 tells us, "And the seventy returned again with joy, saying, Lord, even the devils are subject unto us through thy name. 18 And he said unto them, I beheld Satan as lightning fall from heaven. 19 Behold, I give unto you power to tread on serpents and scorpions, and over all the power of the enemy: and nothing shall by any means hurt you. 20 Notwithstanding in this rejoice not, that the spirits are subject unto you; but rather rejoice, because your names are written in heaven."

Without Jesus, our names would not be written in Heaven, and because of this, I am grateful, and you should be grateful too.

There is a chorus that says, "Oh Lord, I am very, very grateful for all you have done for me. Oh Lord, I am very, very grateful. I am saying thank you, Jesus."

"Thank you, Jesus," are words we should all be saying right now for all that he has done for us.

I Cor 15:50-58 says, "Now this I say, brethren, that flesh and blood cannot inherit the kingdom of God; neither doth corruption inherit incorruption. 51 Behold, I shew you a mystery; We shall not all sleep, but we shall all be changed, 52 In a moment, in the twinkling of an eye, at the last trump: for the trumpet shall sound, and the dead shall be raised incorruptible, and we shall be changed. 53 For this corruptible must put on incorruption, and this mortal must put on immortality. 54 So when this corruptible shall have put on incorruption, and this mortal shall have put on immortality, then shall be brought to pass the saying that is written, Death is swallowed up in victory. 55 O death, where is thy sting? O grave, where is thy victory? 56 The sting of death is sin, and the strength of sin is the law. 57 But thanks be to God, which giveth us the victory through our Lord Jesus Christ. 58 Therefore, my beloved brethren, be ye steadfast, unmovable, always abounding in the work of the Lord, forasmuch as ye know that your labour is not in vain in the Lord."

There is coming a day when death will be swallowed up in victory, and we will rejoice because of what Jesus has done for us!

Romans 8:32-37 tells us, "He that spared not his own Son, but delivered him up for us all, how shall he not with him also freely give us all things? 33 Who shall lay anything to the charge of God's elect? It is God that justifieth. 34 Who is he that condemneth? It is Christ that died, yea rather, that is risen again, who is even at the right hand of God, who also maketh intercession for us. 35 Who shall separate us from the love of Christ? shall tribulation, or distress, or persecution, or famine, or nakedness, or peril, or sword? 36 As it is written, for thy sake we are killed all the day long; we are accounted as sheep for the slaughter. 37 Nay, in all these things we are more than conquerors through him that loved us."

Today, because of the love of God for us, we are more than conquerors through Christ Jesus our Lord. Glory Hallelujah!

In the divine verses of Psalm 92:1 and Colossians 2:13-15, gratitude and triumphant victory resonate, highlighting the transformative power of Jesus Christ. Without Him, sins linger unforgiven, and spiritual adversaries prevail. Luke 10:17-20 underscores the authority bestowed upon believers, urging joy not only in conquering spirits but in our eternal names inscribed in Heaven. The verses caution against rejoicing in earthly pursuits, emphasizing the enduring significance of Christ's love. With hearts full of gratitude, we join the chorus, proclaiming, "Oh Lord, I am very, very grateful!" Anchored by 1 Corinthians and Romans, we anticipate a day of universal rejoicing for the unparalleled victory through our Lord Jesus Christ. Today, standing in God's love, we are more than conquerors through Christ Jesus our Lord. Glory Hallelujah!

29

Away with Him, Away with Him!

Don't push Jesus away; welcome Him as your
Lord and Savior today.

Sometimes in life, innocent people are wrongly imprisoned and murdered, while criminals, murderers, thieves, and those inciting rebellious disorder are set free. This is what happened to Jesus, the King of kings and the Lord of lords. However, the only way for these individuals to escape eternal judgment after death is to repent, come back to Jesus, and follow Him.

Luke 23:18-21 tells us, "And they cried out all at once, saying, Away with this man, and release unto us Barabbas. 19 (Who, for a certain sedition made in the city, and for murder, was cast into prison. 20 Pilate, therefore, willing to release Jesus, spake again to them. 21 But they cried, saying, Crucify him, crucify him."

This Bible passage reveals the final words and decisions made against Jesus before He was sent to Calvary, where He was crucified. Pilate and Herod found nothing in Him worthy of death, but the voices of the multitude and the high priests eventually prevailed, and Barabbas, a thief, murderer, and one who incited rebellious disorder, was released in His stead.

Luke 23:33-43 tells us, "And when they were come to the place, which is called Calvary, there they crucified him, and the malefactors, one on the right hand, and the other on the left. 34 Then said Jesus, Father, forgive them; for they know not what they do. And they parted his raiment, and cast lots. 35 And the people stood beholding. And the rulers also with them derided him, saying, He saved others; let him save himself if he be Christ, the chosen of God. 36 And the soldiers also mocked him, coming to him, and offering him vinegar, 37 And saying, If thou be the king of the Jews, save thyself. 38 And a superscription also was written over him in letters of Greek, and Latin, and Hebrew, This Is The King Of The Jews. 39 And one of the malefactors which were hanged railed on him, saying, If thou be Christ, save thyself and us. 40 But the other answering rebuked him, saying, Dost not thou fear God, seeing thou art in the same condemnation? 41 And we indeed justly; for we receive the due reward of our deeds: but this man hath done nothing amiss. 42 And he said unto Jesus, Lord, remember me when thou comest into thy kingdom. 43 And Jesus said unto him, Verily I say unto thee, Today shalt thou be with me in paradise."

This man was saved in the last few minutes of his life because he believed in Jesus and repented. You still have time to repent and believe in Christ before your candle goes out.

Ephesians 2:4-9 tells us, "But God, who is rich in mercy, for his great love wherewith he loved us, 5 Even when we were dead in sins, hath quickened us together with Christ, (by grace ye are saved;) 6 And hath raised us up together, and made us sit together in heavenly places in Christ Jesus: 7 That in the ages to come he might shew the exceeding riches of his grace in his kindness toward us through Christ Jesus. 8 For by grace are ye saved through faith; and that not of yourselves: it is the gift of God: 9 Not of works, lest any man should boast."

The thief on the cross is a perfect example of what it means to be saved by grace.

Ephesians 2:10 tells us, "For we are his workmanship, created in Christ Jesus unto good works, which God hath before ordained that we should walk in them."

This means that if you did not have the thief on the cross experience, as a believer, you are expected to do good while you are still alive. This is not only a commandment but also your purpose.

Mark 12:28-34 tells us, "And one of the scribes came, and having heard them reasoning together, and perceiving that he had answered them well, asked him, Which is the first commandment of all? 29 And Jesus answered him, The first of all the commandments is, Hear, O Israel; The Lord our God is one Lord: 30 And thou shalt love the Lord thy God with all thy heart, and with all thy soul, and with all thy mind, and with all thy strength: this is the first commandment. 31 And the second is like, namely this, Thou shalt love thy neighbour as thyself. There is none other commandment greater than these. 32 And the scribe said unto him, Well, Master, thou hast said the truth: for there is one God; and there is none other but he: 33 And to love him with all the heart, and with all the understanding, and with all the soul, and with all the strength, and to love his neighbour as himself, is more than all whole burnt offerings and sacrifices. 34 And when Jesus saw that he answered discreetly, he said unto him, Thou art not far from the kingdom of God. And no man after that durst ask him any question."

Some individuals who are not in the kingdom of God know more about what it takes to be in the kingdom of God than those who are already in it. Love for God and love for your neighbor are fruits that should be visible in the life of a believer because, without them, we cannot inherit eternal life.

Luke 13:23-28 tells us, "Then said one unto him, Lord, are there few that be saved? And he said unto them, 24 Strive to enter in at the strait gate: for many, I say unto you, will seek to enter in, and shall not be able. 25 When once the master of the house is risen up, and hath shut to the door, and ye begin to stand without, and to knock at the door, saying, Lord, Lord, open unto us; and he shall answer and say unto you, I know you not whence ye are: 26 Then shall ye begin to say, We have eaten and drunk in thy presence, and thou hast taught in our streets. 27 But he shall say, I tell you, I know you not whence ye are; depart from me, all ye workers of iniquity. 28 There shall be weeping and gnashing of teeth when ye shall see Abraham, and Isaac, and Jacob, and all the prophets, in the kingdom of God, and you yourselves thrust out."

Now, I am not the brightest person in the world, but I am pretty sure that you cannot thrust someone out of something when they are not in it. You cannot thrust a person out of a car if they are not in it. You cannot thrust a person out of an organization if they do not belong to it. And you cannot thrust someone out of the kingdom of God if they are not in it.

John 3:16 tells us, "For God so loved the world, that he gave his only begotten Son, that whosoever believeth in him should not perish but have everlasting life."

If you have never given your life to Jesus, repent, give your life to Him, be baptized, and follow Him.

In conclusion, the profound events surrounding Jesus, Barabbas, and the thief on the cross serve as powerful reminders of the grace, mercy, and love that God extends to all humanity. The sacrificial act of Jesus on Calvary's cross exemplifies the unparalleled gift of salvation by grace through faith. As believers our purpose extends beyond personal redemption; it encompasses a call to live a life of love, good works, and adherence to the commandments of loving God and our neighbors. The urgency to enter through the strait gate and the sobering reality of being thrust out for iniquity should prompt us to examine our hearts. Let the love of God and the transformative power of His grace guide our actions, ensuring that we strive to emulate Christ and, in doing so, secure our place in His eternal kingdom.

30

The Consequences of Pride and Presumptuous Sin

Pride and presumptuous sin are grave matters that can lead to destruction and eternal consequences. God's Word warns us to humble ourselves and avoid these sinful attitudes.

Proverbs 8:13 reminds us that God detests pride, considering it evil in His eyes. To help illustrate the perils of pride, let's explore examples from the Bible.

Example 1: King Nebuchadnezzar - A great and powerful king who initially failed to acknowledge that God ruled over the kingdoms of men. Nebuchadnezzar attributed his success solely to his abilities, leading God to decree his removal from his kingdom. He lived among animals for seven years until he learned that the Most High God appoints rulers, Daniel 4.

Nebuchadnezzar's pride stemmed from ignorance, but once he humbled himself before God, he was restored to his kingdom.

Example 2: Belshazzar - The son of Nebuchadnezzar witnessed his father's humbling experience but failed to heed the lesson. Instead, he desecrated sacred vessels, praising gods that could neither see, understand, nor hear. Consequently, a heavenly decree was issued, leading to Belshazzar's death after seeing a mysterious inscription on the wall, Daniel 5.

Belshazzar was a prideful fool whose unrepentant attitude led to his tragic downfall.

Example 3: The People of Judah and Jerusalem - The inhabitants of Jerusalem, including kings, priests, and prophets, succumbed to pride fueled by rebellion. They disregarded God's guidance, followed their hearts' desires, and worshipped other gods. Therefore, God decreed their intoxication and potential destruction unless they humbled themselves.

Their pride manifested as rebelliousness, refusing to heed divine instructions despite knowing what was right.

Example 4: Egypt's Pride - Egypt's pride was linked to its power and might. However, the message in Ezekiel 30:1-6 prophesied Egypt's downfall and the collapse of her supporters, emphasizing that even the powerful must humble themselves before God.

The lesson here is that no amount of power can protect one from God's judgment if pride remains unchecked.

Presumptuous Sin - Presumption stemming from pride leads to sin. The Bible, in Numbers 15:27-31, distinguishes between sins committed in ignorance and those done presumptuously. Presumptuous sin, whether by native-born Israelites or strangers, is met with severe consequences. Such individuals will be cut off, akin to a branch severed from a tree.

Eternal Consequences - Finally, the consequences of pride and presumptuous sin extend beyond earthly punishments. Revelation 20:11-15 paints a vivid picture of the Great White Throne judgment. Those whose names are not found in the Book of Life face eternal separation from God and are cast into the Lake of Fire, the second death.

In conclusion, pride and presumptuous sin carry severe consequences both in this life and in the afterlife. The Bible encourages repentance, acceptance of Jesus, baptism, and following Him to receive the gift of eternal life or repentance and coming back to Jesus. As Romans 6:23 reminds us, "For the wages of sin is death, but the gift of God is eternal life through Jesus Christ our Lord.

31

Repent and Give your Life to Jesus

John 3:16 states, "For God so loved the world, that he gave his only begotten Son, that whosoever believeth in him should not perish, but have everlasting life."

Everlasting life is promised to everyone who believes in Jesus, but everlasting condemnation is promised to everyone who does not believe in Jesus. So, what does believing in Jesus mean? Believing in Jesus means acknowledging that he is the Son of God, the Savior who redeems the world from sin.

John 3:17 adds, "For God sent not his Son into the world to condemn the world, but that the world through him might be saved."

Moreover, to believe in Jesus implies trusting in his teachings and following him.

I once overheard a conversation among women discussing another woman. They mentioned that this woman "believes in her husband," indicating that she follows his instructions faithfully. When you believe in someone, you place enough trust in them to obey their guidance.

Similarly, when you believe in Jesus, you place your trust in him to follow his guidance and adhere to his written word. Believing in Jesus involves following the promptings of the Holy Spirit.

John 10:27-28 declares, "My sheep hear my voice, and I know them, and they follow me: 28 And I give unto them eternal life; and they shall never perish, neither shall any man pluck them out of my hand."

If you have not yet surrendered your life to Jesus, now is the time to do so. Repent, invite him into your life, undergo baptism and sanctification, and follow his teachings. Additionally, if you recognize that you have backslidden, it is time to repent and return to Jesus.

Apostle O. Michael is a dedicated Servant of the Lord and author who has penned a collection of transformative books aimed at inspiring and guiding readers on their spiritual journeys. Below are some of his notable works:

- "The Power of Jesus Over Depression"
    - In this powerful book, Apostle O. Michael explores how the teachings and presence of Jesus can bring healing and hope to those struggling with depression, offering a path to emotional and spiritual restoration.

- "Remember This Word"
    - "Remember This Word" is a profound exploration of the timeless wisdom found in the Word of God. Apostle O. Michael encourages readers to reflect on and internalize the divine truths that can bring clarity, purpose, and faith into their lives.

- "The Mind of God Towards Your Service"
    - Delve into the mind of God and discover His purpose for your life and service through this insightful book. Apostle O. Michael provides guidance on aligning your actions with God's divine plan.

- "Come Back To Jesus"

- In a world filled with distractions and temptations, "Come Back To Jesus" serves as a spiritual compass, calling readers back to their faith and a deeper relationship with Christ. Apostle O. Michael offers encouragement and practical steps for returning to the loving arms of Jesus.
-

You can find these books at leading bookstores and online retailers.

ABOUT THE AUTHOR

Apostle O. Michael is the founder of Worldwide Prophetic Evangelical Ministries. He passionately spreads the gospel to nations, dedicated to imparting the truth of the kingdom of God and unveiling God's intentions to His people through counseling and prophecy. A devoted servant of the Lord, Apostle O. Michael is happily married and blessed with children. You can watch his insightful videos on YouTube, and for further inquiries, feel free to reach him at michael@wpems.org. Explore more about his ministry at www.wpems.org.

* 9 7 9 8 8 6 9 0 8 5 9 2 4 *